An Introduction to Photoshop Elements 10

Robert Penfold

Bernard Babani (publishing) Ltd
The Grampians
Shepherds Bush Road
London W6 7NF
England

www.babanibooks.com

Please note

© 2011 BERNARD BABANI (publishing) LTD

First Published - December 2011

British Library Cataloguing in Publication Data
A catalogue record for this book is available from the British Library

ISBN: 978 0 85934 730 3

Cover Design by Gregor Arthur
Printed and bound in Great Britain for Bernard Babani (publishing) Ltd

Preface

Digital photography was for many years "just around the corner". Digital cameras were always going to be the runaway success of the next Christmas, but for some years it never quite happened. With hindsight it is easy to see that the early digital cameras were too low in specification and high in cost, and were never going to be a mass marketing success. Some of us began to wonder if high quality and affordable digital cameras would ever appear in the shops.

Things have changed in recent years though, and it is now possible to obtain inexpensive digital cameras that are capable of producing large prints of high quality. These cameras can be used in a very simple manner if preferred, with the memory card containing the pictures being taken to a photo processing shop in much the same way that a film is taken for processing and printing. However, digital imaging gives the photographer far more control than is possible with film photography, enabling huge improvements to be made to photographs after they have been taken. If photographs do not come out as you expected, it is no longer necessary to just "grin and bear it".

Of course, in order to fully exploit digital photography it is necessary to have a computer running a suitable image editing program. Photoshop Elements has for some years been the most popular software of this type, and with good reason. For a relatively low cost it provides a huge range of facilities that cover practically all the software requirements of someone involved in digital imaging. It has facilities for organising digital photographs, editing them in a range of simple and more sophisticated ways, and then using them in various ways such as creating photo albums and calendars.

This book is not intended to make you an expert at using Photoshop Elements 10. It provides brief coverage of the organiser and output sections of the program, but it is primarily concerned with editing digital photographs to give improved results. The emphasis is on the everyday editing tasks that will need to be performed routinely in order to optimise your photographs. The topics covered include correcting colour casts and exposure problems, sharpening "soft" images, adding special effects, undertaking basic retouching, cropping images, correcting distortions of various types, removing purple fringing and providing red-eye reduction. No previous knowledge of digital photography is assumed, but the reader does need to know the fundamentals of using a computer running a modern Windows operating system.

Robert Penfold

Trademarks

Adobe Photoshop and Photoshop Elements are either trademarks or registered trademarks of Adobe Systems Inc. Microsoft, Windows, Windows XP, Windows Vista and Windows 7 are either registered trademarks or trademarks of Microsoft Corporation.

All other brand and product names used in this book are recognised trademarks, or registered trademarks of their respective companies. There is no intent to use any trademarks generically and readers should investigate ownership of a trademark before using it for any purpose.

Contents

3

Selections and layers 83

Organise
and share

Getting organised

This book is primarily about using the main editor of Photoshop Elements to optimise digital images, but some of its other features will be considered, albeit quite briefly, in this chapter. You are greeted with a panel that offers two options when Photoshop Elements is launched. These are to Organise or Edit your photographs, and the two functions are catered for by two separate but linked programs. The Edit option is covered in Chapters 2 and 3, and will not be considered further here. The organiser program is used to upload images to your computer, locate and view digital images that are already stored on your computer, and to make them easier to find months or even years later. It can also be used to load images into the editor program, although they can also be opened from within the editor in the normal way. Thus it is not essential to use organiser as a front end to the editor, and you may prefer to use the editor on its own and make your own arrangements for organising images stored on your PC.

Figure 1.1 shows the main screen of the organiser. The main panel is used to display a scrollable catalogue of photographs, and in Figure 1.1 some pictures have already been loaded. A single image can be viewed by double-clicking its thumbnail (Figure 1.2). There is the usual menu bar at the top, and to some extent this duplicates features that can be accessed via other parts of the user interface. Just below the menu bar there is a toolbar, and left-clicking the arrow at the left end of the bar takes things back to the thumbnail view. To the right of this there is a search facility, and a drop-down menu of various search options. Other buttons allow images to be rotated or viewed in full-screen mode, and there is a slider that controls the size of the thumbnail images. Along the bottom of the screen there is a status bar which tells you the name of the current catalogue and the number of images it contains.

The Task Pane covers the right-hand section of the screen, and it is divided into two sections. These are called Albums, and Keyword Tags. The

*Fig.1.1 The initial screen of the organiser with some photographs
loaded into the catalogue*

panel itself can be resized horizontally, and the three sections can be
resized vertically or minimised/expanded using the arrow buttons at the
top left-hand corner of each one. The Task Pane can be switched off via
the Window menu to maximise the screen area for displaying albums
and images. To create the shell of a new album it just a matter of left-
clicking the green "+" button, supplying a name for the new album, and
operating the Done button. An icon for the new album should then appear
in the Album panel. An album can be deleted by left-clicking its icon
followed by the red "−" button.

There are additional options available from the green "+" button, and
one of these is Smart Album. An album of this type is one that will search
for images that are tagged with a certain keyword. For example, there
could be numerous bird photographs stored in a variety of folders. A
smart album could look for any photographs tagged with the word "robin".
Even though the matching files could be in a dozen or more folders,
they would still be gathered together in a single smart album. An Album
Category is a group of albums with a common theme, such as places,
birds, cars or people, and there is an option for creating a new one. The
From File option can be used to import an album structure.

In order to populate an album with photographs you right-click on its
entry in the Task Pane and then choose the option to edit it from the pop-
up menu. The Task Pane then shows the contents of the album, and it

*Fig.1.2 A single image viewed in the main panel. A caption can be
typed into the area beneath the image*

will initially be blank of course. Images are added to the album by
dragging them in from the main panel. The normal Windows methods
of multiple selection can be used to add several images at once. Left-
click the Done button when you have finished. The editing option can
be used again if you need to add more photographs to an album, or if
you need to remove some. To delete an image from an album it is first
selected by left-clicking its thumbnail, and then the "–" button near the
bottom of the Task Pane is operated.

Loading images

It is obviously necessary to load images into the main panel before they
can be placed in an album. The quick way to load images from the hard
disc into the organiser is to use the menu system to select the searching
method (Files – Get Photos and Videos – By Searching). This produces
the window of Figure 1.3 where you have a limited amount of control
over the drives/folders that the program will search. A common problem
with programs that search for media files on a computer is that they tend
to find vast numbers of files that are used by Windows and application
programs. These are not your personal media files, but will be treated
as if they were.

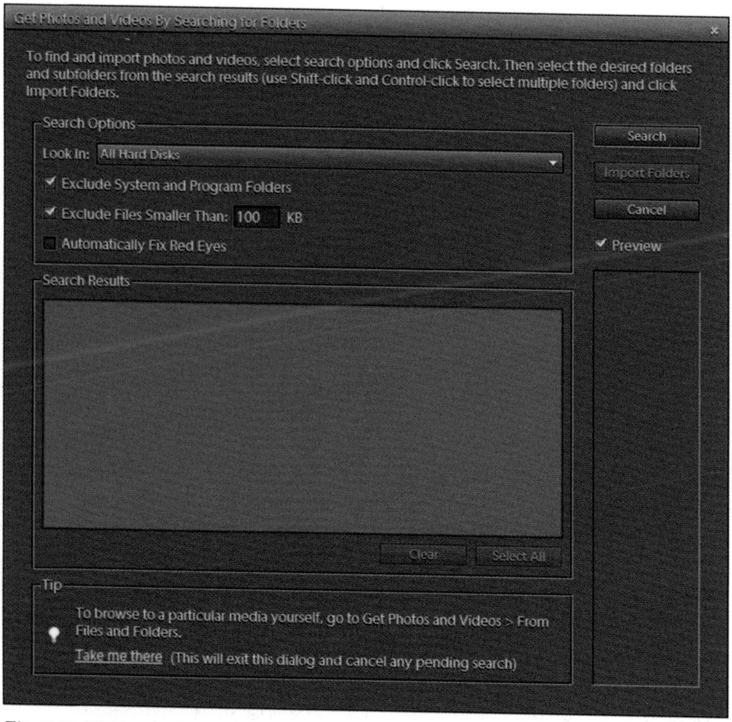

Fig.1.3 *This window gives some control over the images that will be loaded*

To some extent this problem can be avoided here by specifying that files of less than a certain size should be excluded, and that system and program folders should be excluded from the search. The more reliable method is to select the images yourself by launching the files browser (Files – Get Photos and Videos – From Files and Folders). Using the normal Windows file selection methods it can be used to choose a single file, several files, a folder, or even several folders and any subfolders. Assuming your image files are grouped together on the hard disc it should therefore be easy to select and load. However, initially it might be best to select a few dozen photographs to help familiarise yourself with the organiser.

The Get Photos and Videos submenu has options for loading new files from a camera or scanner. It is not essential to do things this way, and new image files can be uploaded onto the hard disc in the normal way and then imported into the organiser if preferred. In fact you do not have to import them manually, since the organiser has a watch facility (Files – Watch Folders) that can be set to automatically import new image files. The Pictures folder and any subfolders are monitored by default, but a location can be specified if necessary.

Tags

Tags are keywords that are used to describe a photograph so that you can search and sort your images. There are some default Tag categories already present in the Keywords Tags section of the Task Pane. New categories, subcategories, and tag keywords can be added via the corresponding options in the menu produced by using the green "+" button. Tagging images is rather like adding images to an album. You drag from the Tag Keyword pane to the target image. The normal multiple section methods can be used with both the tags and the target images. To the left of each icon in the Tags Keywords pane there is a grey button, and operating one of these will result in images that have the corresponding tags being displayed in the main panel.

There are other ways of sorting images. If you go to the Windows menu and select Timeline, a timeline will be displayed at the top of the main panel (Figure 1.4). The vertical bars show the positions on the timeline where there are images available, and the height of each bar gives an indication of the relative number. Left-clicking on a bar results in the images from that period being displayed in the main panel. You can use the Search facility, which will search filenames for strings of characters that match your search term. The Find menu offers numerous additional ways of locating images.

Stacks

Thumbnail images can be stacked on top of each other in the main panel to conserve space. This is mainly done where there are a number of very similar images. In order to produce a stack it is just a matter of using the normal methods of multiple selection to choose the images, right-clicking one of them, selecting Stack from the pop-up menu, and then choosing Stack Selected Photos from the Stack submenu. Left-clicking the arrow button at the right edge of a stack expands it again. A stack can be collapsed again by right-clicking any thumbnail in the stack and selecting Collapse Stack from the Stack submenu. A stack can be undone by right-clicking any of its thumbnails and choosing Unstack

*Fig.1.4 A timeline for the catalogue can make it easier to locate the
required photographs*

Photos from the Stack submenu. There is also an option here for
removing an individual photo from its stack.

Most users will probably settle for using a single catalogue, but it might
be advantageous to have two or more catalogues if you have, or will
have, a very large number of images on your computer. In order to keep
things more manageable there could be separate catalogues for (say),
family photographs, travel pictures, and wildlife shots. A new catalogue
is produced by selecting Catalogue from the File menu. Operate the
New button in the dialogue box that appears, and add a new name for
the catalogue in the textbox. To switch from one catalogue to another,
again go to the Catalogue option in the Edit menu. Select the required
catalogue from the list in the dialogue box and then operate the Open
button.

Fix

There are four tabs at the top of the Task Pane, and as one would probably
expect, Organise is used by default when entering the organiser. The
Fix tab provides access to some basic editing facilities that will be applied
to the selected picture or pictures. Further editing facilities are available
via the pop-down
menu produced by
left-clicking the arrow
at the right end of the
Fix button. There are
quick and guided
editing options, and
one that provides
access to the full
Photoshop Elements
editor. In Figure 1.5 I
have selected an
image from the
catalogue and left-
clicked the Crop

Fig.1.5 Cropping an image

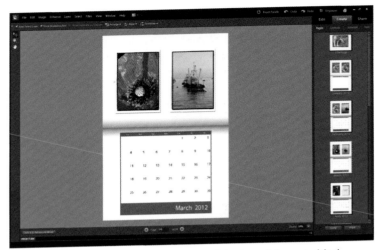

Fig.1.6 Creating a calendar using one of the templates provided

option in the Task Pane. Some types of processing are immediately applied to the selected image or images, but with something like cropping a certain amount of input from the user is required and a small editing window pops up. The basic editing facilities are fine for very simple tasks and as an easy introduction to image editing, but only the full editor enables the full power of Photoshop Elements to be exploited. Note that it is often impossible to undo editing done outside the full editor.

Create

Photoshop Elements has the usual printing facilities so that you can print images at the required size and orientation, and the editing facilities enable cards, calendars, etc., to be produced. However, creating anything other than simple prints can be quite time consuming. The facilities available via the Create tab make it quick and easy to produce a range of things such as calendars, CD jackets, greetings cards and photo books.

Selecting one of the options under this tab results in the full editor being launched. Before entering the editor it is necessary to select the desired layout from a range of templates. There is an option to have the selected pictures in the organiser automatically loaded into the new calendar, photo book or whatever, or the pictures can be added once into the editor. Figure 1.6 shows a calendar being produced in the editor.

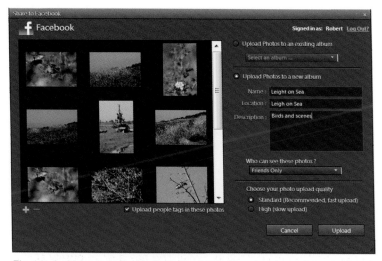

Fig.1.7 In order to upload photographs to Facebook you have to do little more than select the photographs

Share

The Share tab provides a range of options such as producing email attachments, producing an album for use on Flickr, and uploading photographs to your Facebook account. Obviously it is necessary to have suitable online accounts in order to utilize some of these facilities, and with others you need a compatible email client. With the video oriented options it is necessary to have the Premier Elements video editing software installed in order to use them.

They can save a great deal of time if you have the appropriate setup to use the options under the Share tab. Any form of sharing on the Internet tends to involve reducing image files from a few megabytes each to (typically) less than a tenth of a megabyte. Files are automatically reduced to an appropriate resolution and file size when one of the sharing options is selected. For example, in order to upload photographs to your Facebook account it is just a matter of selecting the images, left-clicking the Facebook option in the Share panel, authorising the program to access your account, and using the dialogue box of Figure 1.7 to set things up in the required manner. Photoshop Elements will produce suitably resized files and upload them to Facebook. Of course, the original files are left untouched by this process.

Global editing

Home improvements

Although it has other features, I think it is fair to say that the vast majority of Photoshop Elements users buy the program for its image editing facilities. It is not essential to do any editing of digital images, and there is no point in editing perfectly good images just for the sake of it. However, it is usually necessary to do at least a small amount of editing in order to get the best possible results from a digital camera. These days the average desktop PC is quite powerful and has a good quality colour display, making it well suited to photo editing. A good laptop or notebook computer should also work quite well in this application, although the relatively small screen size is less than ideal.

The camera manufacturers are now starting to include some image editing facilities in their digital cameras, but some photo editing software and a PC is needed in order to do the job really well. Adobe's Photoshop Elements is the front runner at the budget end of the market, and it offers an incredible range of features for the money. It tends to be regarded as a stripped down version of the professional version of Photoshop, but it is really a different program that has been tailored to suit a different market. It is aimed specifically at users of digital cameras who require a program that will enable them to optimise their photographs quickly and easily.

For the professional user it is a matter of "time is money", and some of the features that originated in Photoshop Elements have found their way into the professional version of Photoshop. Photoshop Elements offers many of the features found on expensive professional programs costing about ten times as much, and should certainly be capable of producing some high quality results provided the initial images are not hopeless cases.

It is important to realise that although Photoshop Elements is a very capable program, there are images that are hopeless cases, and no computer program can work miracles. Remarkable improvements can often be made to images that have poor technical quality, but no photo editing program can bring out detail, colour or other information that is

Fig.2.1 The default layout for the editing screen

simply not there in the original image. It is often possible to make artistic improvements to an image that is lacking in this respect, but again, it is unlikely that great improvements can be made to a picture that has no artistic merit. The idea is not to take awful pictures and then make them great using photo editing. You should aim to get the best possible pictures, both artistically and technically, and then where necessary, make them even better with Photoshop Elements.

Basics

When the initial screen of Photoshop Elements appears, selecting the Edit option produces a screen like the one shown in Figure 2.1. The screen layout is in most respects fairly standard for a modern Windows program, with a conventional menu bar at the top and a toolbar down the left-hand side of the screen. The large area to the right of the toolbar is used to display the picture that is being edited. There are areas to the left of and below the picture area that can be used to provide quick access to other pictures and certain features of the program, as will be described later.

The entire editing screen is known in Photoshop terminology as the "workspace", and although it looks like Figure 2.1 by default, it can be customised to suit individual requirements. Existing elements of the layout can be switched off or moved, and new ones can be switched on. As you learn to use Photoshop Elements it is virtually certain that changes to the workspace will be introduced, and you may well alter the workspace quite frequently as you customise it to suit different projects.

All the usual features are available via the menu bar, which has some standard Windows menu headings. It provides access to the usual facilities under the File menu, including Open, Save, and Print options. There is also a New option, which generates a blank picture area of the required size. It is possible to use Photoshop Elements as a paint program to create your own onscreen masterpieces, starting with a blank page, but it is not primarily aimed at this sort of thing. Other options are available from the New submenu, and these are mainly means of merging several photographs, to produce a panoramic picture for example. There is also an option that effectively opens an image that is stored on the Windows clipboard.

Undo/Redo

There are some buttons at the right-hand end of the menu bar, including Undo and Redo buttons that are very useful. These duplicate but provide quick access to the Undo and Redo options in the Edit menu. As is now the case with many Windows programs, these are of the multi-level variety. In other words, if you do four or five pieces of editing and then change your mind, it is just a matter of using the Undo button four of five times in order to remove the unwanted changes. If you should then change your mind again, using the Redo button four or five times will reintroduce the changes.

This is important, because it gives users the freedom to make changes, happy in the knowledge that these can be easily undone if they simply do not like the changes, or if it all goes disastrously wrong. There is a limit to the number of steps that can be undone and redone, and the default limit is 50 steps. The reason for having a limit is that storing details of each step uses the computer's resources, and in particular it can grab large amounts of the computer's memory.

It is possible to alter the maximum number of steps that can be undone by selecting Preferences from the Edit menu, and then choosing Performance from the submenu that appears. In the Preferences window (Figure 2.2) the History states can be set in the range 2 to 1000, but remember that using a high number could hog the computer's resources and result in things operating at greatly reduced speed once a large amount of editing has been undertaken. It could be beneficial to set a

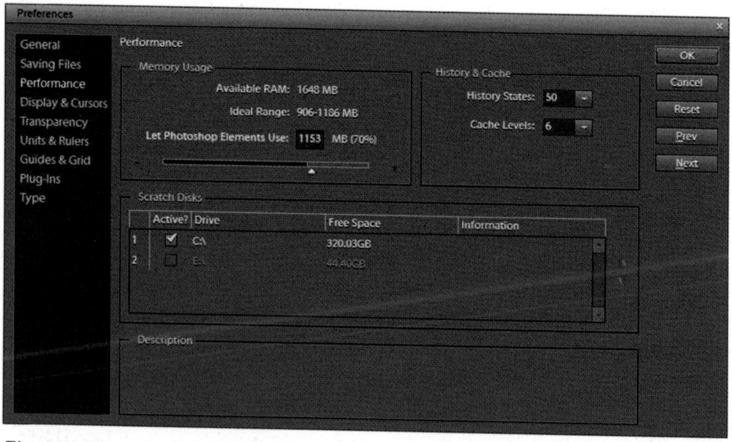

Fig.2.2 The maximum number of History states can be altered here

lower figure if you are using a computer that is equipped with a relatively small amount of memory.

Menus

Some of the other menus are the type of thing found in many Windows programs, such as Edit, Help, Window and View. The others mainly provide access to editing features that are applied to the entire picture, or to a previously selected portion of the picture. The toolbar down the left-hand side of the screen also provides various editing facilities, but these are more selective in nature. For example, there are tools for selecting an area or several areas of the picture that can then be processed in some way, or for painting onto the picture in various ways.

There are various zoom options available under the View menu, but there is also a magnifier tool available in the toolbar, which is often the best choice when zooming in to examine part of the picture in detail. Not surprisingly, the magnifier tool is the one that has a picture of a magnifying glass as its icon (the second button from the top). As usual with toolbars, some hint text will appear if you place the pointer over an icon, and this tells you the function of the tool. In order to use the magnifier tool it is just a matter of using the mouse to drag a rectangle that covers the area of interest. That area will then fill the display area, which is the large blank section of the screen to the right of the toolbar.

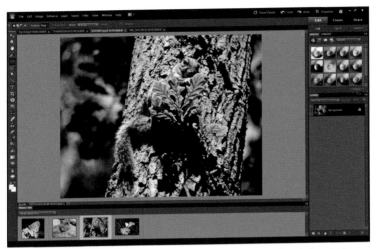

Fig.2.3 The Project has a thumbnail for each picture that is loaded

Perhaps the most important of the zoom options in the View menu is the one called Actual Pixels. This zooms in on the image to an extent that results in each pixel of the image being matched to a single pixel of the displayed image. The point of using this feature is that it does not involve any of the compromises that usually occur when scaling an image up or down in size. You see a true representation of the image that is as accurate as your computer's display system can manage. When you need to assess the technical quality of an image, and particularly when judging its sharpness, the Actual Pixels view is all-important.

The problem with the Actual Pixels view, or any zooming in on the image, is that it is unlikely to fit into the area of the screen reserved for the picture. With something like a low resolution image for use on the Internet it is possible that it will fit into the display area for the picture, but the image from any reasonably modern digital camera is likely to be far too large. The number of pixels in the display area depends on the video generator and monitor you use, but it is unlikely to be more than about one million pixels.

Even the digital cameras of about ten years ago produced larger images than that, and today's digital wonder cameras usually have pixel counts in the 10 to 20 million range, and some exceed the 20 million mark. You can still view the full image, and choosing the Fit On Screen option from the View menu will result in the current image being displayed in its entirety and as large as possible in the available space.

Panning

Photoshop Elements has a real-time pan feature that makes it easy to explore a zoomed image. This is accessed via the Hand tool in the toolbar, which you will probably not be surprised to learn is the one that has a hand icon on its button. There is a useful keyboard shortcut to this tool, which is to press the spacebar. The Hand tool will remain active for as long as the spacebar is pressed. The real-time panning feature operates in a manner that is a bit like having the full image behind a small window that enables only part of the image to be seen at any one time. The display area is the window, and the Hand tool enables the image to be dragged so that the desired section can be viewed.

As with most Windows programs, Photoshop Elements can have more than one file at a time loaded into the computer's memory and ready for editing. There is an area below the display section of the screen called the Project Bin, and this shows a so-called "thumbnail" for each image file that has been opened. In other words, it shows a miniature version of each image (Figure 2.3). In order to make an image the active one in the display area it is just a matter of double-clicking its thumbnail in the Project Bin.

Of course, it is by no means essential to make use of this feature, and there are potential advantages in not doing so. Bear in mind that each image loaded into Photoshop Elements uses some of the computer's resources, and in particular, uses up the memory. This is unlikely to be a problem when dealing with low resolution images for use on the Internet, but could well be of significance when editing high-resolution images from something like an 18 megapixel camera. Unless you really need to have several images loaded simultaneously it is better to edit them one at a time and to switch off the Project Bin via its entry in the Windows menu. Its area of the screen then becomes part of the picture area. When required again it can be switched on by selecting Project Bin from the Windows menu.

Any section of the screen listed in the Windows menu can be toggled off and on in this way. A tick next to one of the menu entries indicates that the relevant window is active, and selecting it from the menu will result in that window being switched off. The relevant window is currently inactive if a menu option does not have an accompanying tick, and selecting an option will then switch on that window.

Fig.2.4 The Fit on Screen zoom setting displays the picture as large as possible

There is a control bar immediately beneath the menu bar, and this is extremely important. The controls and options it offers are dependent on the particular tool selected from the toolbar, and it greatly increases the versatility of most tools. If you find that a tool is not operating in the expected manner it is likely that something in this control bar is not set correctly.

Panel Bin

The right-hand section of the screen is called the Panel Bin, and it provides easy access to features such as filters, effects, and layers, but only when the Edit tab is active. The features on offer here depend on the settings in the relevant section of the View menu, and the ones shown in Figure 2.1 are those that are selected by default. You can add the colour swatch window for example, by selecting the relevant option in the View menu. This whole section of the screen can be switched on and off via the Panel Bin entry in the View menu. The features available from the Panel Bin will be considered in later sections of this book.

The Create and Share sections of the program used to have options in the initial menu screen that appears when the program is launched. However, in the current version they are accessed by selecting Edit from

Fig.2.5 A full-screen option is available in the Organiser

the initial menu screen, and then selecting the appropriate tab in the right-hand section of the editing screen. We will not consider the Create and Share sections of the program any further here, as they were covered separately in the first chapter of this book.

Full screen?

There would seem to be no full screen viewing option in the editing section of Photoshop Elements. You can close any active panels and then use the Fit on Screen option or other zoom controls from the View menu to display the picture as large as possible (Figure 2.4). This gives a reasonably detailed view of the picture, but it is using something less than the full capabilities of the monitor.

In order to get the best possible view of the picture it is necessary to first save the edited picture. Then launch the organiser section of Photoshop Elements, and there is a button for this purpose near the top right-hand corner of the screen. Once in the organiser it is just a matter of loading the appropriate file and then switching to the full screen mode (Figure 2.5).

Instant results

Most programs that have some photo editing tools can provide a quick fix using some form of automatic editing facility. This will usually try to correct the exposure, maximise the contrast and correct any colour cast. As one would probably expect, an automated system of this type does not always get everything absolutely right, and sometimes produces results that look ridiculous. The program providing the processing does not know whether the picture is of a group of people or a sunset, and the generalised rules it uses will not suit widely differing subject matter. On the other hand, there is no harm in trying automated processing. It provides a quick and easy solution when it works, and the processing can be instantly removed if the end result is useless.

Automatic correction works best when the subject matter is something fairly ordinary, and when the source images only need slight adjustment. It tends to be least effective with images that are unusual in some way, such as being predominantly one colour, and where a large amount of processing is required. With images that are well out of the ordinary, such as those of very low-contrast scenes, the program will probably take the out of the ordinary aspect to be a fault and will try to correct it. A low contrast scene will be given a full range of tones and will probably look quite ridiculous. With images that need a lot of processing it will be necessary for the program to take a number of what are effectively guesses at the required processing, and it is quite likely to get it wrong at least once.

Auto Smart Fix

Photoshop Elements has several types of automatic processing, but the one that provides an all-in-one fix is the Auto Smart Fix type, which is the first entry in the Enhance menu. As the "Smart" part of the name suggests, this system of automatic processing does not just apply a few simple rules when attempting to optimise an image. It analyses the image and then makes adjustments that are dependent on the result of this analysis. With a high resolution image and a computer that "is not as young as it used to be" it might take several seconds for the process to be completed. Note that with any lengthy image processing task you can cancel the process at any time by pressing the Escape (Esc) key.

Although the Auto Smart Fix feature applies some clever programming when processing an image, it is still far from one hundred percent reliable. With a program running on a PC that must complete the task in a

Fig.2.6 This photograph is obviously far too dark

reasonable amount of time it is inevitable that the process will still to some extent be a bit "hit and miss". It should be borne in mind that only you know what the finished image should look like, and Photoshop Elements cannot mind-read.

The butterfly photograph of Figure 2.6 has an obvious problem in that it is underexposed and is therefore far too dark. As a result of this the contrast is also quite low, and on my monitor at least, the colours do not look quite right. Applying the Auto Smart Fix produced the improved image of Figure 2.7. Although this version is undoubtedly better, with improved brightness and contrast, it is still far from right.

It is still rather dark, although to some extent this is simply due to the fact that the original image was taken using flash and this has darkened the background. This is because the butterfly and the flower were very close to the flashgun, while the background was much further away and was therefore lit far less strongly. It is difficult to compensate for this type of thing convincingly, and it is probably best to settle for a dark background. It does not matter too much in this case because the flower and butterfly

Fig.2.7 Auto Smart Fix has partially corrected the picture

stand out quite well against the dark background, and it could even be considered an advantage.

The butterfly and the flower are a little darker than would be ideal, and if anything, the colour balance of the image has been adjusted in the wrong direction. A slight excess of blue has been accentuated, and is most noticeable in the small light areas of the butterfly which are far too blue/ violet in colour. The yellow flowers have a greenish tinge, which also suggests a blue cast. Probably the cause of this problem is that the image has large areas of yellow, brown and orange, which the program has interpreted as a slight yellow/orange colour cast. In attempting to correct this it has introduced a blue/green cast.

Even if the Auto Smart Fix does not produce a perfect image, it will often improve things and make it easier to "fine tune" the picture manually. It only took a few seconds to manually adjust the image of Figure 2.7 to produce the finished picture of Figure 2.8. The image has been lightened some more, and the amount of blue has been reduced. This gives a result that might not be perfect technically, but is the way I think the

Fig.2.8 Some manual adjustment has further improved the picture

image should look. It helps to keep in mind that photo-editing is not about achieving theoretical perfection, but is a way of getting images to look the way you think they should look. In some cases this might involve filters and special effects that give an end result that has little in common with the original scene!

It is possible to apply some control over the Auto Smart Fix processing, but the only aspect that can be controlled is the strength of the applied processing. This alternative version is obtained by selecting Adjust Smart Fix from the Enhance menu, and a small window with a slider control will then appear on the screen (Figure 2.9). Using the slider it is possible to vary the amount of processing from zero to one hundred percent, but the level of processing produced by the standard version of Auto Smart Fix seems to equate to about fifty percent and not one hundred percent. The amount of processing provided can therefore be weaker or stronger than that provided by the normal version.

Where the Auto Smart Fix processing is essentially correct, but it needs to be slightly stronger or weaker, the adjustable version enables the

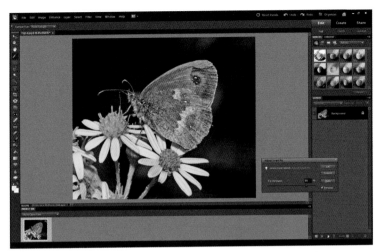

Fig.2.9 The Adjust Smart Fix facility will not necessarily produce improved results

processing to be fine tuned. It should then provide an excellent final image. It will probably not be of much help if the processing is fundamentally flawed in some way. In Figure 2.9 I have used one hundred percent processing on the butterfly picture, which has lightened it further, but the excess of blue in parts of the picture has been accentuated to such a degree that it is into the realms of special effects!

Auto Levels

Auto Levels is another form of automatic quick fix that can be accessed via the Enhance menu. This is a more simple form of automatic adjustment than the Auto Smart Fix type, but this does not necessarily mean that it will always provide inferior results. In some cases the simple approach is all that is needed. Unfortunately, in other cases it can provide hopeless results, and applying Auto Levels processing to the butterfly picture has not given particularly good results (Figure 2.10). The yellow flower looks slightly "washed out" and should be a much stronger yellow colour. The slightly bluish parts of the butterfly are a strong blue/violet colour, and in this respect results are very similar to those in Figure 2.9.

The photograph of Figure 2.11 is the type of image that is likely to work well with automatic processing. Technically it is more or less right, even though the contrast is very low and there is a slight blue cast. These are

Fig.2.10 Using Auto Levels has again given a partial improvement

caused by the picture being taken some distance away from the subject matter using a telephoto lens, and on a day that was slightly misty. The half a mile or so of mist between the camera and most of the subject matter has reduced the contrast and given a slight colour cast. This accurately reflects the way things were when the picture was taken, but it does not really give a particularly good image. Some mistiness in a photograph can help to give atmosphere and a pleasing effect, but this is not really the case here. It was a bright day with strong vibrant colours, but the use of a telephoto lens has resulted in a rather drab picture.

Figure 2.12 shows the same picture after processing with Auto Smart Fix. Using Auto Levels instead produced a very similar result. The main effect of the processing is to boost the contrast and give a less misty looking picture, but the amount of blue has also been reduced slightly so that the greenery in the foreground has greener greens. There is still plenty of mist in the background, helping to give the image a feeling of depth.

Fig.2.11 Automatic processing should work well with this picture

Fig.2.12 The automatic processing has produced a significant improvement. The excessive haze has gone and the colours are much better

Fig.2.13 This picture is too dark and the contrast is low

Auto contrast

In addition to all-in-one fixes, Photoshop Elements has separate systems for automatically adjusting the contrast and making colour corrections. When an automatic system fails completely it is usually because the automatic colour correction has made things worse instead of better. We have already seen the Auto Smart Fix and Auto Levels facilities have this problem in the examples of Figures 2.7 and 2.10. Being as charitable about it as possible, any automatic colour correction feature is likely to be of limited practical use, but an automatic contrast facility is extremely useful. It provides a very quick and easy way of ensuring that a photograph has a full range of tones.

There are various causes of a photograph lacking a full range of tones, and in some instances it is simply that the subject matter is genuinely low in contrast. Often it is due to slight over or under exposure making the photograph generally too bright or too dark. It is quite common for digital cameras to err slightly in the direction of under exposure. This is not due to a fault, and it is the way they were designed to operate.

Slight overexposure results in detail being lost in the burned-out highlights, and no amount of processing will recover the missing detail. A small amount of under exposure will presumably lose a certain amount

Fig.2.14 Using the Auto Contrast facility has improved matters

of detail in the darkest parts of the image, but in practice it is usually possible to "lift" a lot of detail from the dark areas of the picture. After a certain amount of processing it is quite likely that a slightly under exposed picture will look fine, but the same is not true of slightly over exposed pictures.

The photograph of Figure 2.13 is not too bad, but it has rather low contrast and is a bit dark. Sometimes there is an obvious cause of the problem, such as a large area of bright sky that has "fooled" the camera's automatic exposure system and left the foreground too dark. Here it just looks like a straightforward case of under exposure due to "pilot error". Using the automatic contrast system of Photoshop Elements produced the image shown in Figure 2.14, which has boosted the contrast and lightened the picture a little. It might benefit from some further work, but it is a big improvement on the version of Figure 2.13, and is quite good as is.

Over the top

An automatic contrast facility will not always provide the desired effect, and it is not something that should be used with a photograph that quite correctly contains something less than a full range of tones. For example, the misty scene of Figure 2.15 has a rather limited range of tones, but

Fig.2.15 *This picture of a boat in the fog quite correctly has a low level of contrast*

this is only to be expected with a scene of this type. The image gives the impression that it was a very dull day with plenty of mist and fog around, and it was. The picture is perhaps a little drab, but the lack of contrast is correct.

Fig.2.16 The effect of using Auto Contrast is "over the top"

Boosting it to a full range using an automatic contrast system provided the result shown in Figure 2.16. This version is more dramatic, but it does not really have a great deal in common with the original scene. The mist in the middle distance and foreground has miraculously

Fig.2.17 The Contrast and Brightness controls

disappeared! Using high contrast on a low contrast scene will often give a more dramatic or prettier picture, but it will not be a true representation of the original scene, or anything approximating to it.

Brightness/Contrast

Where more subtle changes in brightness and (or) contrast it is necessary to resort to manual adjustment, and Photoshop Elements has conventional brightness and contrast controls. These are available from the Enhance menu by selecting Adjust Lighting and then Brightness/Contrast. There are slider controls for adjusting the brightness and contrast (Figure 2.17), and it is really just a matter of using trial and error to find the settings that give the best result. The two settings interact in a way that often results in a great deal of going to and fro between the two controls before you finally end up with the desired result.

In Figure 2.18 I have tweaked the brightness and contrast slightly in an attempt to add a little more contrast and tame the brightness. The changes are not that great, but it gives a finished result that is much closer to the way I remember the original scene. The boat stands out a little more from the background, and the yellow colour of its hull, which was all but lost in the original image, is more noticeable.

Darkening

Figure 2.19 shows another shot of the two butterflies, but this has the opposite problem to the previous one. The camera was accidentally knocked from auto to manual exposure, and this has resulted in an overexposed image. Fortunately, the degree of overexposure is not very high, but it has resulted in the picture being generally too light. Also, some of the brightest areas are burned out to pure white. There is nothing that can be done about this second point, but the main areas that have become burned out are shiny parts of leaves that are reflecting the bright sky. There is no detail of importance in these areas, and they still give the right effect in that the leaves still look shiny.

Fig.2.18 The manually adjusted version of the photograph

With an overexposed photograph of this type the Auto Contrast facility will generally darken the picture, hopefully revealing some extra details in the brighter parts of the picture as part of this process. In this example the change is minimal (Figure 2.20) and some further processing is required. One way of tackling the problem is to take the fully manual

Fig.2.19 *This image is slightly overexposed*

Fig.2.20 *Auto Contrast has only given a slight improvement*

Fig.2.21 The Highlight control has been used to darken the highlights

approach using brightness and contrast adjustments. However, using the Highlights control is usually quicker and easier, and mostly gives excellent results.

The Highlights control is accessed via the Enhance menu (Adjust Lighting – Shadows/Highlights). There are actually three controls on the small control panel that this produces (Figure 2.21), and the Lighten Shadows control will be advanced to fifty percent by default. In the current context this will almost certainly make matters much worse rather than better, so it should be set it at zero. The Midtone Contrast control is simply ignored, and the Darken Highlights control is advanced to give the desired result. In Figure 2.21 I have advanced it enough to bring out a little more detail in some of the lighter areas, and this slightly darker version of the picture is a little easier on the eye when viewed on a large computer monitor.

Colour saturation

When editing photographs, and particularly when making adjustments to the brightness and contrast, there can be problems with the colour saturation. Looking at things as simply as possible, the colour saturation is the strength of the colours. Weak colours that have low saturation are effectively diluted with grey, giving them a rather washed out appearance. Strong colours have high purity and are very lively. When making

Fig.2.22 Using minimal saturation produces a monochrome image

adjustment to the brightness and (or) contrast of an image you will often find that there is an apparent reduction in the general degree of colour saturation. Less commonly, the colours might seem to become excessively strong.

Photoshop Elements has a colour saturation control that is available via the Enhance menu (Adjust Color – Adjust Hue/Saturation). There are actually three slider controls in the pop-up Hue/Saturation panel (near the bottom right corner of the screen in Figure 2.22), but for the moment we will only consider the Saturation control, which is the middle one. It is a bit like a volume control for colour, and taking it fully to the left removes the colour altogether and gives a monochrome image, as in Figure 2.22. Taking the saturation control further to the right produces stronger colours, but it is best not to get carried away and produce images that have so-called "Mickey Mouse" colours. Taking things still further can sometimes give very odd looking results.

In Figure 2.23 I have advanced the Saturation control slightly in order to strengthen the colours, which it has done. The saturation control operates in a very simple manner, and the problem with adding saturation to the weaker colours is that it also boosts those that are already quite strong. This has certainly occurred in this example. Using the saturation control is often a matter of selecting a good compromise between strengthening

Fig.2.23 Here the Saturation control has been advanced slightly

the weaker colours on the one hand, and avoiding excessively boosting the medium and stronger colours on the other hand.

The slider beneath the Saturation control is the Lightness control, which despite its name can be used to lighten or darken an image. It is useful to have the Saturation control and the Lightness one on the same control panel since you can make changes to the brightness and then immediately make any necessary adjustment to the saturation level. With a certain amount of going to and fro from one control to the other it should be possible to quickly obtain the desired result. In theory, lightening an image will often require the saturation to be increased slightly, and reducing the brightness will usually require a small decrease. Things do not necessarily work this way in every instance though, and it obviously applies only when the colour saturation level is about right to start with.

Vibrance and RAW

Photo editing software often has a vibrance control, which is a more sophisticated version of the saturation type. Rather than treating all areas of colour equally, a vibrance control has more effect with weaker colours than those of medium saturation, and it has little or no effect with areas

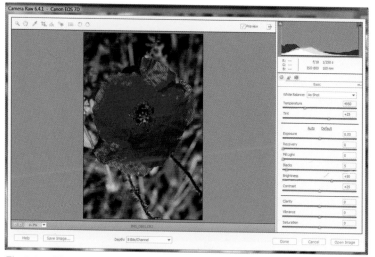

Fig.2.24 There is a Vibrance control in the Camera RAW add-on

where the colour saturation is high. This makes it possible to boost weak colours without sending the stronger areas of colour "over the top". A vibrance control is usually designed to have little effect with skin tones. This makes it possible to boost or reduce the colour saturation of other elements in a picture without making the people look either very ill or extremely embarrassed!

Unfortunately, there is no vibrance control in Photoshop Elements, but there is one in the free Camera RAW add-on. This add-on is primarily intended for use with RAW files, which are an option on the more upmarket digital cameras. A RAW file is basically just the raw data from the camera's sensor. It will not have undergone any form of processing in the camera such as changes to the white balance. RAW files are preferred by photographers who require the highest possible picture quality, because RAW files are not compressed, and do not have the loss in quality associated with compressed image formats such as the ever popular JPEG type.

One drawback of RAW files is that they are relatively large. One of my cameras produces RAW files that are about 25 megabytes per file. The highest quality JPEG files it produces are around 6 to 7 megabytes per file. Another problem with RAW files is that they are not a standard format like JPEG, TIFF, and other image files. A RAW file has a format that is

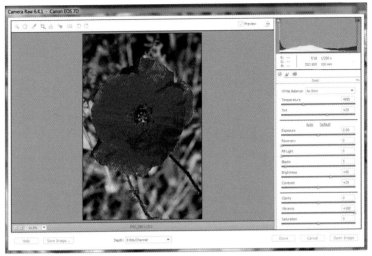

Fig.2.25 The effect of advancing the Vibrance control

tailored to suit the sensor on the particular camera that produced it. There are not only differences from one manufacturer to another, but even the cameras from a given maker have different RAW formats. This is not a major problem with the Adobe Camera RAW add-on, as it can handle RAW files from a huge range of cameras. However, there can be a significant delay between a new camera being released and the Camera RAW add-on being updated to accommodate it.

Opening a RAW file in Photoshop Elements results in a new editing window appearing (Figure 2.24), and this has a useful range of controls that cover brightness, colour saturation, and so on. The Vibrance control is second from bottom, above the Saturation control. In Figure 2.25 the vibrance level has been set at maximum, and in Figure 2.26 it is at zero. Notice how most of the colour has been removed in Figure 2.26, but the picture has not been converted into a black and white type. The strong reds in the petals of the poppy have been changed very little, giving an interesting effect for those who like that type of thing.

Once the required adjustments have been made in the Camera RAW add-on you can operate the Done button to save the changes and exit the program. Operating the Open Image button also saves the changes, but it then opens the image in Photoshop Elements, where it can be edited in the normal way, and then saved in the desired picture format

Fig.2.26 Strong colours are retained at zero Vibrance

such as JPEG or TIFF. Note that changes made to an image in the Camera RAW add-on do not alter the RAW file. Non-destructive editing is used with RAW files, which means that the RAW file itself remains unchanged, and details of the editing are stored in a companion file when the changes are saved. Of course, when the file is opened in Photoshop Elements it is not actually the RAW file that is being opened. A new file is generated and this can be saved in the usual way, and the normal way of operating then applies. You then have the original RAW file, a file containing the changes made using the Camera RAW add-on, and the file or files saved after editing the image in Photoshop Elements.

Camera RAW and JPEG

It is actually possible to open a JPEG file in the Camera RAW add-on, and its range of controls, including the vibrance one, can then be used to edit the image. A JPEG file is opened in the Camera RAW add-on by first launching Photoshop Elements, and then selecting Open As from the File menu. This produces the usual file/folder browser which is used to select the required image file. Select Camera RAW from the Open As menu, and then open the file. This will produce the Camera RAW program, complete with the opened JPEG file (Figure 2.27).

Fig.2.27 A JPEG image opened in the Camera RAW add-on

The required changes are then made to the image, which can be loaded into Photoshop Elements using the Open Image button. The file can then be edited further if required, and then saved in the usual way. The Camera RAW add-on is quite a powerful image editing program, and it is a useful option to have available, even if you do not use RAW files.

Colour balance

Often problems with the colours in an image are not due to an error in the saturation levels, but are instead due to a more fundamental problem. Severe problems with colour are more likely to be due to a colour cast. Digital cameras have various white balance options, but most users just settle for the automatic option. These are generally quite good at assessing the prevailing light and setting a suitable white balance so that the pictures displayed on the screen of your monitor reflect the way things looked when the picture was taken.

On the face of it, there is no need for any adjustments to the colours in a photograph, and everything should be fine if the camera simply records things the way they were. In practice it is not as simple as that. Tungsten lighting has a strong red content when compared to typical daylight, and fluorescent lighting is usually quite green in colour. You tend not to notice this when you are in a room that is lit by either of these light sources, because your eyes and brain adjust to the colour of the lighting and accept it as normal.

If you take a photograph using either of these types of artificial light they will probably not look right to most people unless some adjustment is made to the colours. The colours may well be true to the originals, but on the photograph they are being viewed out of context by people who have not adjusted their perception to match the conditions when the photograph was taken. A picture taken under tungsten lighting will look too orange/red, and one taken under some form of fluorescent lighting will tend to look too green, probably with some rather odd looking colours being produced.

A camera's automatic white balance system tries to produce natural colours that will look right when you view the photograph on the screen of a computer or in the form of a print. This feature has to be regarded as something of a mixed blessing. In the right context it will have the desired effect, but it will sometimes kill the mood of an image. Natural light can be quite blue on a dull day or when there is a blue sky but the sun is obscured by cloud. At sunrise and sunset it can be very red in colour due to the filtering effect of dust particles in the sky. At other times it can be anywhere between these two extremes. These different colours of light give a scene atmosphere, and the automatic white balance feature of a camera can sometimes alter the colour balance and totally change the mood of an image. The reds and oranges of a sunset can be altered to give a picture that has the sun near the horizon, but otherwise looks as if it was taken at midday!

Digital cameras usually have alternatives to an automatic white balance control. One of these should be a natural setting, where the white balance is left untouched. When you are trying to capture the mood of a scene this is usually a better option than an automatic white balance control, and it can avoid having to correct the corrections made by an automatic white balance system. Use the automatic system when the lighting is in some way unusual and is likely to need some correction in order to obtain natural looking results.

Auto colour

Photoshop Elements can provide automatic colour adjustment, but like the automatic white balance feature of a camera, it will not always provide the desired result. There is no harm in trying this feature, since it can be undone using the History palette or the Undo facility. Photoshop Elements

Fig.2.28 Automatic Color Correction tends to produce "cold" results

does not know whether the image is a seascape or a bunch of flowers, a spectacular sunset or a predominantly green cricket pitch at midday, so an automatic colour balance facility inevitably involves some technical guesswork. Sometimes it will be right or quite close, but often the results will be a long way out.

In order to try out this feature it is just a matter of going to the Enhance menu and selecting the Automatic Color Correction option. This feature is fully automatic, and it is not possible to make any manual adjustments. Applying automatic colour correction to the picture of the two butterflies produced the result shown in Figure 2.28. The photograph was taken on a summer's day in the late afternoon, which is why the original image is rather yellow in colour. This helps to give the picture a summery feel, and is not something that needs to be corrected. The yellow cast of the original image is perhaps a little strong, but this is better than the version of Figure 2.28 where the colours are rather "cold", and the bluish colour balance has lost the summery feel of the original. In general, automatic colour correction facilities tend to produce a rather "cold" colour balance.

Fig.2.29 This image has a slight blue/green tint

The Auto Color Correction facility has worked better in Figure 2.29 where the image has a slight blue/green tinge. Automatically correcting the colours has produced the better result of Figure 2.30. The difference is not huge, but it has tamed the slightly unnatural colours in the sea and the sky. Of the two images, the version of Figure 2.30 certainly looks more like the original scene.

Remove Color Cast

The Remove Color Cast function offers a very quick and simple way of removing a colour cast, It is accessed via the Enhance menu, and it is the first option in the Adjust Color submenu. It operates in conjunction with the Eyedropper tool, and the pointer will change to an eyedropper icon when this option is selected. The basic idea is to indicate a point on the image that should be black, white, or a mid-grey, but actually has a colour cast. Photoshop then automatically adjusts the colour balance of the image so that the selected spot is the right colour, and this should remove the colour cast from the image.

Fig.2.30 Automatic Color Correction has produced better colours

This method is not totally reliable in practice, since it is dependent on the user finding a spot on the image that should be pure black or white, or a neutral grey. Finding a suitable medium grey is quite difficult, and there may not be a suitable colour on the image. Most images have something very close to pure black or white, or what would be pure black or white if there was no colour cast, and using one of these is a more practical option. However, an area that looks as though it should be black or white may actually have slight coloration. This colour will be removed by the processing, and the whole image will be given the same treatment. The colour cast will not be accurately counteracted, and a new colour cast will be introduced.

Of course, if things do not go perfectly the first time another spot on the image can be used as the reference point. You can try different reference points as often as you like in an attempt to get it right, but with some images there may be no suitable reference areas.

The photograph of Figure 2.31 shows a spider on a bluebell flower, but the bluebell is perhaps not quite as blue as it might be. Despite their name, bluebell flowers do in fact have a significant amount of violet colouring and are not what might be considered true blue in colour.

Fig.2.31 *This picture has a slight red cast*

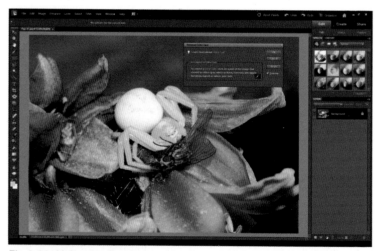

Fig.2.32 *Using the Eyedropper tool on a highlight has improved matters*

Fig.2.33 Sampling an unsuitable point will give poor results

However, in this case there is a bit too much violet and the picture has a slight reddish cast. In Figure 2.32 I have applied the Eyedropper tool to a highlight on one of the spider's legs. This has produced the desired effect, with the bluebell flowers being much bluer in colour. The colour shift has not been overdone, and the areas that were previously more violet in colour have retained a tinge of violet. Things can easily go wrong if you are not careful enough with your choice of reference point. In Figure 2.33 the reference point was taken from an area that was almost black but seemed to have a slightly red colour cast. Unfortunately it has excessively reduced the amount of red in the picture, and has produced a strong colour cast. In general, using an almost white reference point is easier than using one that is mid-grey or almost black.

Color Variations

Color Variations is another option in the Adjust Color submenu, and it also provides a relatively simple means of adjusting the colour balance. The photograph of Figure 2.34 has some lovely strong blues in the body of the damselfly, which is not surprising as the whole image seems to have a bluish colour cast. The greens in the leaves for example, should be a mid or slightly yellowish green, but are actually a blue - green colour.

Fig.2.34 The problem in this case is a mild blue cast

Selecting the Color Variations feature produces the pop-up window of Figure 2.35. The top section of the window shows the original image and the modified version, but these will be the same initially. The lower section of the window shows six variations that have extra red, green, and blue, and reduced amounts of these colours. It is possible but unlikely that one of these variations will be exactly what is required. In that event, it is just a matter of left-clicking on the appropriate version, and the modified image will then adjust to match it. Operate the OK button to return to the image and make the changes take effect.

In most cases some adjustments will be required in order to get a really good colour balance. The basic colour casts are quite strong, but they can be weakened or made even stronger by adjusting the slider control near the bottom left-hand corner of the window. Left-clicking on one of the tinted images two or three times is another way of obtaining stronger effects. You are not limited to one type of correction, and can also left-click on different images to combine two tints. For example, rather than substantially reducing the amount of blue or increasing the amount of red, you could use both, but to a lesser degree.

Left-clicking on the lighter and darker images in the bottom right-hand section of the window respectively lightens or darkens the modified

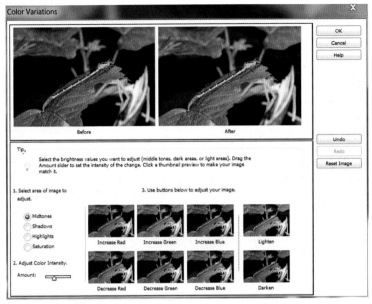

Fig.2.35 The Color Variations window

image. Again, left-clicking two or three times gives a stronger effect, and the slider control can be used to vary the amount of change per mouse click. With both the colour balance and the brightness you can either settle for something that is not totally adequate but is passable, or you can gradually "fine tune" the image until it is exactly as required.

It is just a matter of left-clicking on the unmodified image if you would like to remove all the processing and start again from scratch. The OK button is operated when the desired effect is obtained, or the Cancel button is operated if you change your mind and wish to abandon the processing. In this example I settled for decreasing the blue level by a modest amount and slightly lightening the image, giving the result shown in Figure 2.36.

There are four radio buttons near the bottom left-hand corner of the window, and three of these enable the mid-tones, shadows or highlights to be adjusted. The default is for the mid-tones to be adjusted, which is usually all you will need to do, but the other two options are there if you need them. There is also a Saturation option here, and the window

Fig.2.36 The blue level has been reduced slightly

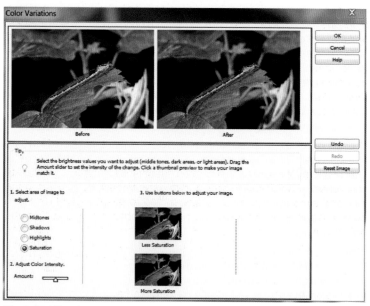

Fig.2.37 The degree of colour saturation can also be changed

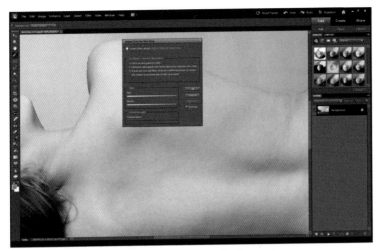

Fig.2.38 The skin tones in this image are far too red

changes to look like Figure 2.37 when this is selected. This operates in much the same way as before, but there are only two thumbnail images, and these give increased colour saturation (the bottom one) or decreased saturation (the top one). The slider control enables the amount of change to be varied. It is useful to have a colour saturation control available from within the colour variations feature, but it provides a rather clumsy method of control. For most purposes the ordinary colour saturation control is a more convenient way of handling things.

Skin tones

One of the most difficult aspects of colour balance is obtaining accurate skin tones. Photoshop Elements has an automatic system for doing this, and although it cannot be guaranteed to provide good results in every case, it is certainly worth trying. It is obtained by selecting the Adjust Color submenu from the Enhance menu, and then left-clicking the Adjust Color for Skin Tone option. A pop-up window then appears (Figure 2.38), and the pointer is automatically switched to the eyedropper mode.

In the example of Figure 2.38 the skin tones have quite a bright pink colour cast, and this gives a slightly unnatural look to the image. In

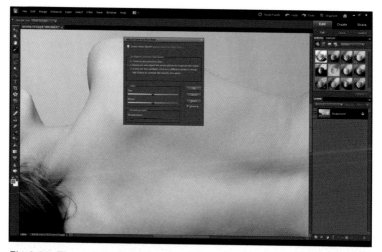

Fig.2.39 The automatic adjustment has produced better skin tones

order to automatically adjust the colour balance it is just a matter of left clicking with the Eyedropper tool on an area of skin tone. There might be a delay of a second or two while the program makes its adjustments, and then the new colour balance will be applied to the entire picture and not just the skin tones.

In this example it has been quite successful (Figure 2.39), and the excessively pink tones have been tamed to give a result that is more natural looking. If you do not like the adjusted colour balance it is possible to have another attempt by first operating the Reset button to restore the original colour balance, and then trying the eyedropper tool on another area of skin tone. This can be tried several times if necessary. Operate the OK button when a suitable colour balance has been obtained, or the Cancel button if you wish to give up and go back to the original settings. Even where the adjusted colour balance is less than perfect, it is probably worth keeping the changes if they are an improvement on the original balance. Some manual adjustments can then be used to "fine tune" the colours and get everything just right.

Adjust Color Curves

This is the Photoshop Elements simplified version of the Curves facility in Photoshop. In Photoshop it is possible to adjust the curves individually

Fig.2.40 The foreground in this picture is far too dark

for each colour channel, but in Photoshop Elements all three channels are adjusted together. Although it is in the Adjust Color submenu of the Enhance menu, it is primarily used as a means of adjusting brightness and contrast rather than altering the colours in an image.

The image of Figure 2.40 will be used for this example. Fairly obviously this image is generally too dark, and the cause of the problem is the massive amount of contrast in the scene being photographed. The difference in brightness between the bright areas of sky and the darkest shadow areas is massive, and is really too much for the camera to accommodate it properly. The camera's exposure system has opted for an exposure value that keeps detail in the sky and other bright areas of the picture, but in doing so it has rendered the mid-tones very dark, and many of the shadow areas are virtually black. Simply increasing the brightness will improve the mid-tone and shadow areas, the brighter areas will go white and any detail they contain will be lost. We need to lighten the shadow and mid-tone areas without lightening the highlights to a significant degree.

Selecting the Adjust Color Curves option launches a new window (Figure 2.41). This has "before" and "after" versions of the image in the upper section of the window. Beneath this in the left-hand section of the window there a scrollable menu of preset curve adjustments. On the other side of the window there is an area that shows the curve, but unlike the

Fig.2.41 Several preset settings provide useful starting points

Photoshop version, it is not possible to directly control the curves by adding points and dragging them. Instead it is controlled by the slider controls in the middle-lower section of the window. These have functions such as making shadows lighter or the highlights darker. This method of control is less versatile than the direct method, but on the other hand it is much easier to use and understand.

When the Curves window is opened there is a noticeable lack of curves. Instead, there is a graph that has a straight line going from the bottom left-hand corner to the top right-hand corner. What is the graph showing? It simply shows the input levels on the horizontal scale versus the output levels on the vertical scale.

As things stand, each input level produces an identical output level, and no processing is applied. The line can be turned into a curve by selecting one of the preset adjustments, other than the Default setting which gives a straight line. It can also be turned into a curve by adjusting one of the slider controls. Using a curve alters the relationship between the input and output values. The zero and 100 percent input levels still produce zero and 100 percent output levels, but changes occur at other levels. For example, bulging the middle of the curve upwards produces an

Fig.2.42 The Shadow control has been used to lighten the foreground

increase in mid-tone brightness. Bulging the line in the opposite direction gives a reduction in mid-tone brightness.

In both cases the change in brightness is achieved without introducing any clipping. Clipping is where areas of the image reach their maximum or minimum values in all three colour channels, giving pure white and black respectively. Any details in the clipped areas will be lost, so it is important to avoid clipping. Unless some pretty wild adjustments are made, clipping will not be introduced when using any form of Curves control.

With the Photoshop Elements version of the Curves control it is probably best not to bother too much about the curves in the graph. It is a matter of selecting the preset adjustment that gives the best result, and then doing some "fine tuning" using the slider controls. In Figure 2.41 I have selected the Increase Midtones preset to provide some general brightening of the picture. The Adjust Shadows slider control has then been used to lighten the shadow areas. This has given the picture a large increase in brightness without introducing any clipping in the blue sky and other bright areas.

Shadows/Midtone Contrast

We saw earlier how the Highlights control can be used to darken highlights in a picture. The same control panel also has Shadow and Midtone

Fig.2.43 The solarized version of the photograph

Contrast controls, and these offer an alternative way of processing a picture that lacks brightness in the shadow areas. In Figure 2.42 I have used the Shadow control to lighten the shadows. Using this control to a significant extent often produces rather "flat" looking images with an apparent lack of contrast.

This is simply due to some of the darker areas being lightened so that they are virtually mid-tones, but the mid-tones are lightened very little. Although the overall contrast of the picture remains unchanged, in many areas of the picture the local contrast is greatly reduced, producing a rather "flat" result. This effect was very pronounced in the example of Figure 2.42, so I used a large increase in the Midtone Contrast control to correct this problem.

Solarisation

One of the preset adjustments in the Adjust Color Curves window gives a solarisation effect (Figure 2.43). As will be readily apparent from Figure 2.43, solarisation is a form of special effect. With film photography it is achieved using one or two tricks when developing a film or making a print. It produces an image that is wholly or (more usually) partially a negative of the original. In other words, some dark areas become light

Fig.2.44 The original colour photograph of the insect

areas, and some colours are changed to their complementary colours. Red becomes green for example, and blue becomes yellow.

The example of Figure 2.43 was made using the standard solarisation settings, with no adjustments added via the slider controls. Some parts of the picture have not changed all that much, with the lightest and darkest areas, if anything, being even lighter and darker. The green areas remain a green colour, of sorts. There are some large changes in the mid-tones though, with blue areas of sky being changed to yellows, oranges and reds. Some of the blue-grey clouds have been changed to brown. Anyway, if you are into this type of thing it is worth trying the solarisation effect.

Convert to Black and White

Photoshop Elements has two facilities for converting a colour image to black and white, and the simpler of the two is the Remove Color option, which is another one in the Adjust Color submenu (Enhance – Adjust Color – Remove Color). It simply uses an average of the colour values for each pixel, which in many cases is all that is needed. This is actually the same as setting the Color Saturation control to zero, as described earlier (see Figure 2.22).

Fig.2.45 The black and white version of Fig.2.44

Using this method on the insect photograph of Figure 2.44 produced the passable result of Figure 2.45. The insect stands out reasonably well from the background, but overall the image is perhaps a little on the dark side. However, if deemed necessary, this could easily be adjusted using the various forms of brightness and contrast control available in Photoshop Elements. The Color Curves facility for example, works more or less normally with black and white images.

A potential problem with the simple approach to black and white conversion is that it can produce rather bland results. Suppose that a picture of a vase of flowers is converted into black and white, and that the flowers are various colours but are all in the mid-tone range. In the black and white version they will all be a mid grey and will all look much the same. A better result would probably be obtained by weighting the conversion so that some colours were converted to relatively dark tones while others were made lighter than normal. This would give viewers the impression that the flowers were different colours, and would give a more lively and interesting picture.

Another potential problem with a basic black and white conversion is that bright colours can be translated into rather drab shades of grey. The photograph of Figure 2.46 has some very bright greens produced by the sun shining through the leaves on the tree. Unfortunately, in the

Fig.2.46 The leaves in this photograph look very bright

Fig.2.47 The monochrome leaves are rather subdued

simple conversion to black and white of Figure 2.47 the effect of the light coming through the leaves has been lost, as has the mood of the original picture.

A more sophisticated conversion to black and white can be obtained by selecting the Convert to Black and White option from the Enhance menu. This launches a new window (Figure 2.48) that shows the usual "before" and "after" images in the upper part of the window. Beneath this on the left there are several preset adjustments on offer. These cover common types of photograph such as portraits and landscapes. On the right there are slider controls for the three primary colours and the overall contrast.

In use the idea is to choose the preset adjustment that gives the best result, and to then do some "fine tuning" with the slider controls if some further improvement is required. For the photograph of Figure 2.46 I selected the Vivid Landscape setting, which produce a good converted image without the need for any further adjustment (Figure 2.49).

Hue control

The Hue control is available when the Adjust Hue/Saturation option is selected from the Adjust Color submenu (Enhance – Adjust Color –

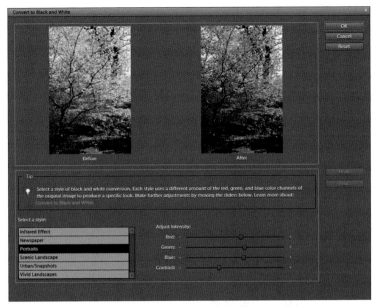

Fig.2.48 Choose the preset that gives the best starting point

Adjust Hue/Saturation). The Saturation control was covered previously in this chapter and will not be considered any further here. The Hue control is a means of altering the colour balance. It can produce subtle changes, massive changes, or anything in between.

I think it is fair to say that the Hue control is a bit confusing. If you try experimenting with various settings it will probably appear to be producing random colour changes. The two colour bars at the bottom of the window were not placed there to make it look pretty, and if you move the Hue control to the right the lower colour bar will shift to the left. The picture of two roses shown in Figure 2.50 is used as the basis of this example, and in Figure 2.51 the Hue control has been moved to the right. This has duly resulted in the lower colour bar being shifted out of alignment to the left. In Figure 2.52 the hue control has been moved to the left, and the lower colour bar has moved to the right.

What the two colour bars are showing are the input and output colours. With the Hue control at a central setting the two bars are aligned and the input colour is always the same as the output colour. Move the control slightly to the left and yellow on the top bar (the input colour) is vertically aligned with orange on the lower bar (the output colour). There is a

Fig.2.49 The leaves are much brighter in this version

Fig.2.50 The rose picture with no adjustments made

similar shift right across the spectrum. Move the Hue control slightly to the right and things are reversed, with orange being replaced with yellow, etc.

Fig.2.51 The colour balance has been shifted in the yellow direction

Fig.2.52 Moving the slider in the other direction gives more red

These small adjustments give what artists term warmer colours if the Hue control is moved to the left or colder colours if it is moved to the right. In other words, more red and more blue respectively. I find this is

Fig.2.53 Extreme settings give a negative colour effect

Fig.2 54 In the original the flower is a purple colour

useful for adjusting skin tones. Skin tones that are too red giving a "lobster" effect can be corrected by moving the Hue control to the right. Slightly green and unnatural skin tones can usually be corrected by

Fig.2.55 The Hue control has been used to change the colour of the flower

Fig.2.56 The flower has been changed to yellow using just the Hue control

moving the Hue control fractionally to the left. More than slight changes produce massive colour shifts, and you are then into the realm of special effects (Figure 2.53). Moving the control fully left or right produces a colour negative, but not a negative in terms of brightness. In other words, the colours are reversed, but light areas remain light, and dark areas will still be dark.

So far it has been assumed that colour and brightness changes will be applied to the entire image, but the Hue control is often used with selected parts of an image. Using the selection tools of Photoshop Elements is covered in the next chapter, and it will not be considered in detail here. In Figure 2.54 the Quick Selection tool has been used to select the flower head, but nothing else. In Figure 2.55 the Hue control has been adjusted to the right, which has resulted in the flower head changing from purple to red. The rest of the image remains unchanged, and the foliage is still green.

The Hue control has a form of built-in selection that can be very useful if you only need to make changes to parts of the picture that are a certain colour. There is a menu near the top of the Hue/Saturation window, and by default this is set to the Master option. This simply means that the Hue control will affect all colours. The menu offers a range of six colours that can be used instead, and changes will then be applied only to the selected colour. Sliders appear on the colour bars to indicate the colour

Fig.2.57 Both types of colour fringing are apparent here

range that will be altered by the Hue, Saturation, and Colour controls. There are two sets of sliders, with the inner pair indicating the range of colours that will be fully altered by adjustments to the controls. The outer pair indicates the colours that will be affected to a lesser extent.

In Figure 2.56 I have selected Magenta from the menu, which is a good match for the colour of the flower head. Since there is nothing else in the picture that is close to the colour of the flower head, I have moved the sliders further apart in an attempt to ensure that all the relevant colours are embraced. Moving the Hue control to the right has turned the flower head yellow/green in colour, but the rest of the image is unchanged. The Saturation and Lightness controls, like the Hue control, will only affect colours within the selected colour range, so I use them to produce a slightly brighter flower head with stronger colours.

Purple fringing

Purple fringing, or chromatic aberration as it is also known, is a problem that occurs with many cameras. It mainly occurs when photographing something that is very dark when there is a bright background, such as the branches of a tree with bright sky in the background. However, with some cameras it can occur in parts of the image where the contrast is relatively low. There is a thin blue or purple area where the light and

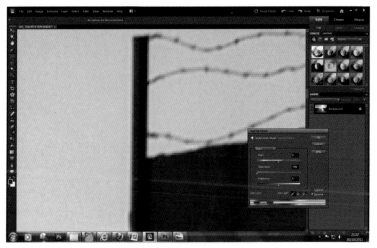

Fig.2.58 The purple fringing has been removed

dark parts of the image meet, and it is from this that the purple fringing name is derived. Although it is termed purple fringing, there are usually two fringes, one on each side of the branch (or whatever). There is a blue/purple fringe on one edge and an orange/yellow one on the opposite edge. In practice the other fringe is often much less obvious though.

The fringing can be on the object in the foreground, in the background, or a bit of both. In the example of Figure 2.57 there is a massive amount of blue/purple down the left-hand side of the wooden post. A highly zoomed view is shown in Figure 2.57 so that it is easy to see the fringing, but it was severe enough to be all too obvious when viewing the entire image on the screen. To remove the purple fringing I launched the Hue/ Saturation control, selected Blues from the menu, and then used the Eyedropper tool at a point on the fringing in order to optimise accuracy. Setting the colour saturation at its lowest value removed the blue/purple colour and made the left side of the post blend in properly with the rest (Figure 2.58).

In this example the yellow/orange fringing on the opposite side of the post is also fairly prominent. It was removed using the same basic technique, but Yellows was selected from the menu. The Eyedropper tool was then used to sample the fringing and optimise the accuracy of the process. Taking the saturation to its lowest level then removed the colour, leaving a much more natural looking post (Figure 2.59).

Fig.2.59 Here the yellow fringing has also been removed

Red-eye reduction

Most digital cameras have a facility to reduce the so-called red-eye effect when taking flash photographs of people using the built-in flashgun. While red-eye reduction features are generally quite effective, they do not guarantee that your photographs will never suffer from this problem. Actually it is not just photographs of people that can fall foul of the red-eye effect, and it can occur when photographing, cats, dogs and many other animals.

It can also happen when the light source is close to the camera, or is shining in the same direction as a light source on the camera. For example, if there is low sunlight coming from behind you, and the subject is just to one side of your shadow, there is a likelihood of the light being reflected off their retinas and back to the camera. Some of the worst cases of red-eye that I have encountered were actually on photographs of animals taken using natural light.

Most photo editing programs have an automatic red-eye reduction facility. In the absence of a human volunteer prepared to be seen in print with glowing red eyes, I have used a photograph of a squirrel for this example (Figure 2.60). Photoshop Elements has automatic facilities for dealing with red-eye, and can remove it when importing photographs. Like most

Fig.2.60 The squirrel is suffering from a case of red-eye

automatic red-eye reduction systems it simple locates the offending red areas and replaces then with black. This is not always totally convincing, and it is often better if the job is done manually using the Hue control.

Fig.2.61 The red in the eye has been desaturated

Fig.2.62 The finished version of the squirrel photograph

Many of the colours in the photograph are similar to the reds and orange colours in the red-eye area. I therefore used the Magic Lasso tool to select the eye of the squirrel before launching the Hue/Saturation control. This ensures that the changes are only applied to the red-eye and that the rest of the photograph is left untouched. In Figure 2.61 I have reduced the colour saturation to zero, which removes all colour from the red-eye area of the image, giving grey-eye rather than red-eye. The Lightness control was then backed off so that the grey areas were darkened, but not so much that they became black. The OK button was then pressed in order to keep the changes and exit the Hue/Saturation control, and then the selection marquee around the eye was removed. This gave the processed image of Figure 2.62, which looks a bit more convincing than the effect obtained when simple converting the reds to black.

Sharpening

Digital cameras tend to produce slightly "soft" images due to the way in which they work. The cameras therefore include built-in sharpening

Fig.2.63 This picture of a raven is slightly" soft"

facilities that counteract this "softness". The built-in sharpening may be all that is required, but some additional processing may be required at times. Also, the best results are not usually obtained by using a lot of in-camera sharpening and then using other forms of processing. If images are likely to receive a fair amount of processing using a photo editing program, results are generally best if little or no in-camera sharpening is used, and the sharpening is applied once all the other processing has been completed.

Some photo editing software, including Photoshop Elements, offers several different types of sharpening, but the basic way in which this effect operates is always the same. Blurring results in light areas producing an increase in the brightness of nearby dark areas, and dark areas causing a reduction in the brightness of nearby light areas. Sharpening effects try to counteract this by providing localised increases in contrast.

Some sharpening facilities have various controls that enable the effect to be optimised for any given image, but getting the best results from this type of thing can be quite difficult. For many purposes a simple automatic system is all that is needed. Photoshop Elements offers a fully automatic method and two types that are controlled manually.

In order to use the fully automatic method it is merely necessary to load the image into the Photoshop Elements editor and then select Auto

Fig.2.64 Automatic sharpening has not made much difference

Sharpen from the Enhance menu. The degree of sharpening provided is not that high, and is often barely noticeable. Figure 2.63 shows the Photoshop Elements editor loaded with a photograph of a raven with a

Fig.2.65 Using several lots of sharpening produces a stronger effect

beak full of peanuts. It has been zoomed using the Actual Pixels option from the View menu, which should always be used when assessing the sharpness of an image. While not totally blurred, it is far from being completely sharp. Using the Auto Sharpen facility has not made a great deal of difference (Figure 2.64), and it is necessary to look very carefully in order to detect any improvement at all.

The image is too blurred for this type of quick fix to be successful. It is possible to use the Auto Sharpen facility two or more times in order to obtain a greater degree of sharpening. Sharpening has been applied four times in Figure 2.65, and this certainly gives a much sharper looking result, but there are some odd effects appearing in parts of the image. The normal problem if too much sharpening is applied is the so-called halo effect. If things are taken too far, the boost in local contrast provided by the sharpening tends to produce white lines close to sharpened edges. Other odd effects can be produced, especially in highly textured areas. Dots of bright colours can appear, and this problem is starting to appear in a few places in Figure 2.65.

Adjust Sharpness

Where more than a small amount of sharpening is required it is best to resort to one of the methods that uses manual control. One of these is Adjust Sharpness, which is an option in the Enhance menu. A new window is launched when this option is selected (Figure 2.66), and the left-hand section shows part of the image at the Actual pixels zoom level.

This shows the effect of the applied level of sharpening, but this will also be shown on the image in the main editing window if the Preview checkbox is ticked, as it will be by default. It is therefore better to have the Adjust Sharpness window out of the way in one corner of the screen. The main display can then be used to monitor the effects of adjustments to the sharpness controls. Using the Preview facility will slow things down, but with any reasonably modern computer it should not become unacceptably sluggish. Note that the Preview option is usually available when some form of control window appears, and that it is always best to use this facility where it is available.

A menu enables three types of sharpening to be applied. The Gaussian Blur option gives the standard version of sharpening, and is a good general purpose option. Lens Blur is used when trying to counteract a lack of sharpness due to a slight lack of resolution from the lens. This is probably the main problem in the Raven picture, which was taken using a powerful telephoto lens, and then the picture was cropped to about

Fig.2.66 The Adjust Sharpness feature gives plenty of control over the sharpening

half its original size. I used the Lens Blur option for this example, but results would probably have been very similar using the Gaussian Blur option. Motion blur is designed to counteract blurring caused by a moving subject or "camera shake". This type of blurring will be considered later in this chapter.

The More Refined checkbox will be ticked by default, and using this feature gives better performance with very fine detail. This is normally an advantage, and it is definitely a good idea to use it with low resolution images, such as those for web pages. The downside of using this feature is that it will tend to increase problems with the sharpening making "noise" in the picture more obvious. "Noise" is the graininess or texture of coloured dots that can sometimes be seen on digital images, especially in plain areas such as expanses of blue sky. It is most severe when using high ISO sensitivities or long shutter speeds. Anyway, if there is a lot of "noise" in an image it might be better to remove the tick from this checkbox.

Having selected suitable options, it is then a matter of using the two slider controls to provide the required sharpening effect. The Radius control determines how far the sharpening will extend from edges, and the Amount Control sets the degree of sharpening used. In general, a low value of about one is used with small images and those that only need a small amount of sharpening. Higher values are used with images

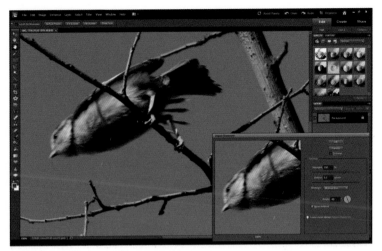

Fig.2.67 Movement has slightly blurred this photograph

that have large pixel counts and (or) there is a fair amount of fuzziness to contend with. However, in practice it is a matter of trying various Radius settings, and adjusting the Amount control for the best results at each of these settings. The right settings are the ones that you deem to give the best subjective result, regardless of whether they conform to the "rules of the game".

On the face of it, the same amount of sharpening should be needed regardless of how an image will be viewed. In practice it is not as simple as that, and it is generally best to err on the side of caution when sharpening an image that will be viewed on a monitor. Even getting slightly carried away will usually result in an image that looks unnatural and obviously sharpened to excess. Presumably due to the lower contrast of a print, a slightly higher level of sharpening often gives the best result, although it is still necessary to use a degree of restraint in order to avoid unnatural looking images.

Motion Blur

Motion blur is cause by movement of the camera or the subject while the exposure is being made. It is not usually a problem when using fast shutter speeds and a wide-angle or standard lens. It becomes more problematic with slow shutter speeds, with powerful telephoto lenses,

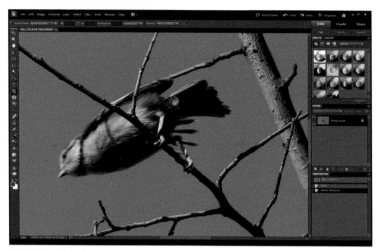

Fig.2.68 The sharpened version of the photograph in Fig.2.67

and when taking close-ups. Modern cameras often have built-in image stabilisation, or use lenses that sport this feature. This reduces the risk of camera shake, but at best you can only go three or four shutter speeds lower before camera shake becomes a problem.

For example, if you would otherwise need to use a shutter speed of one hundredth of a second or faster, with image stabilisation you might be able to get away with 1/15th or 1/8th of a second. Of course, image stabilisation does not help with any movement within the picture. In fact it encourages the use of slower shutter speeds which greatly increase the chances of blurring due to movement of the subject matter.

Anyway, the Motion Blur setting of the Adjust Sharpening facility can help with this type of blurring, but only in minor cases. With severe motion blurring, especially if it gives a double-image effect, there is no effective way of counteracting the blurring. Using this version of the Adjust Sharpening facility is much the same as normal, but there is an additional control for the angle of the blurring (Figure 2.67). You should find that varying the angle produces little effect at some settings and a stronger effect at others. The angle that produces the strongest effect is the one to use.

If the angle control has little effect, either the problem is due to motion blur, or the degree of blur is too great for the sharpening to be of any

Fig.2.69 Unsharp Mask has three slider controls

help. In Figure 2.67 the Preview facility is switched off so that you can compare the original image with the sharpened version in the Adjust Sharpen window, and with the finished version in Figure 2.68.

Unsharp Mask

Unsharp Mask is a more complicated form of sharpening, and a highly regarded one, which is essentially the same as the equivalent feature in the full version of Photoshop. It has three controls (Figure 2.69) in place of the two in the Adjust Sharpening facility. It is accessed by selecting Unsharp Mask from the Enhance menu. The top control is used to set the required amount of sharpening, and the middle control is the familiar radius type.

The third slider control sets the Threshold, which is the difference needed between pixels before the sharpening with be applied. Here we are talking in terms of the difference in contrast needed before it will be accepted as an edge and sharpened. High values result in Photoshop finding few areas to sharpen. With a low value the filtering is applied almost everywhere on the image, which usually results in patterns of dots starting to emerge from previously plain areas of the image. It can take a fair amount of juggling with the three controls in order to obtain the best results, but it should be possible to obtain a reasonably sharp

Fig.2.70 The sharpened version of the photograph in Fig.2.69

looking picture provided the original image contains a reasonable amount of detail. In Figure 2.69 the Preview facility has been switched off so that you can see the original version. Figure 2.70 shows the sharpened picture.

Correct Camera Distortion

Photoshop Elements has a facility that is designed to compensate for deficiencies in the lens of a camera. It is accessed using the Correct Camera Distortion option in the Filter menu. The photograph of Figure 2.71 has a common problem called vignetting, which is the darkening in the corners of the picture. This is something that occurs to some extent with any camera lens, but it is normally kept down to a low enough level to be of no importance. However, with some types of lens it is quite noticeable. The types of lens that are most prone to this problem are very wide-angle types, and zoom lenses that cover a massive zoom range. As one would probably expect, it is more likely to occur with a cheap camera and lens than when using upmarket professional camera equipment. It also tends to be more of a problem with digital cameras that with film types.

It is easily corrected using the two vignette controls in the Correct Camera Distortion facility (Figure 2.72). Moving the Amount slider to the right

Fig.2.71 This photograph has obvious vignetting

lightens the corners, but it might not be possible to find a setting that gives an even level of brightness across the frame. However, it should be possible to obtain reasonably consistent results by adjusting the

Fig.2.72 Vignetting is easily corrected

Fig.2.73 The two trees in the foreground are suffering from a case of converging verticals

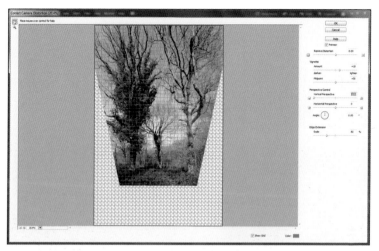

Fig.2.74 The converging verticals can be straightened

Midpoint slider. It is possible to deliberately add vignetting by moving the Amount slider to the left. This effect is often used as a means of concentrating the viewer's attention on the subject matter in the centre of the picture, and distracting them from the background. It is an effect that was often used with portraits in the early days of photography, and it can be used to give a picture and Olde Worlde look.

Converging verticals

The perspective controls can be used to add perspective effects, and they are also useful for correcting a problem known as converging verticals. This problem occurs most commonly when photographing tall buildings. The camera is normally aimed upwards in order to avoid having an excessive amount of foreground and too little building in the shot. This tends to produce a photograph that gives the impression the building is keeling over. The cause of the problem is a standard perspective effect. With the tops of the buildings being much further away than the lower stories, they are smaller and closer together.

In Figure 2.73 the two trees in the foreground show this effect, and they seem to be leaning toward one another. While the two trees were not bolt upright, they were not leaning over in the manner suggested by the photograph. Using the Vertical perspective control it is possible to expand

Fig.2.75 This image has noticeable pincushion distortion

the upper part of the picture and straighten the trees (Figure 2.74). Unfortunately, this leaves triangular shaped blank areas in the lower section of the picture. These can either be cropped or filled using cloning techniques (see Chapter 3).

Distortion

The Distortion control is used to correct pincushion or barrel distortion. The photograph shown in Figure 2.75 is suffering from very obvious case of pincushion distortion. Note how the horizon is far from straight. It curves inwards towards the centre of the picture, which is pincushion distortion. If it curved outwards from the centre it would be barrel distortion. By moving the Distortion slider to the left it is possible to correct pincushion distortion (Figure 2.76). Move it to the right in order to counteract barrel distortion.

Filters

Photoshop Elements has a wide range of effects filters that can be accessed via the Filter menu or via the Effects panel. If it is not currently active, the Effects panel can be switched on using the Effects entry in the Windows menu. There is insufficient space available here for a

Fig.2.76 The curved horizon has been straightened

detailed discussion of the various filters, but this would probably be pointless anyway. The best way to learn about the filter effects is to load

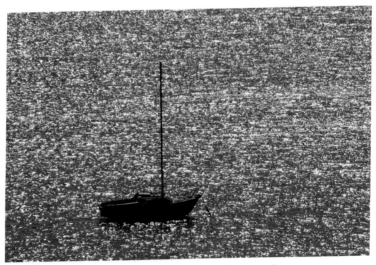

Fig.2.77 The "before" version of the boat photograph

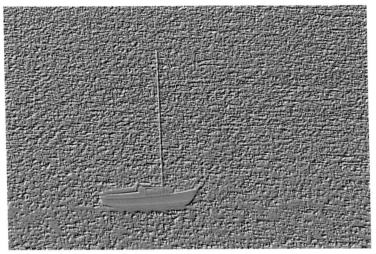

Fig.2.78 The "embossed" version of the boat image

in a photograph and then experiment with them. In most cases there are controls that enable the filtering to be adjusted for the best effect.

Fig.2.79 The image before filtering is used

Fig.2.80   Graphic Pen filtering has been applied to the image

As a couple of examples of filter effects, Figure 2.78 shows the Embossed filter applied to the photograph of Figure 2.77. The idea is to make the image look as though the design is embossed on a sheet of metal, and there is a control for the depth of the embossing. Any colour information in the original image is discarded, which is also the case with the Graphic Pen effect in the image of Figure 2.80. The original version is shown in Figure 2.79. The image has been reduced to numerous thin lines, and there are controls that determine the length and angle of the lines. There is also a control that enables the picture to be lightened or darkened. These two examples are types of artistic filter, but there are other types, such as the posterized flower of Figure 2.81.

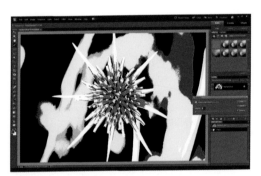

Fig.2.81   A posterised flower

Selections and layers

Cropping

Cropping is where the picture is trimmed at one or more of the edges, and it is one of the most common forms of photo editing. Many cameras have viewfinders that show rather less than actually appears in the photographs, and this even applies to some quite expensive SLR cameras. Consequently, it is often necessary to trim the edges of the image in order to get back to your original composition. Another reason for cropping pictures is that you were not as careful as you might have been when originally framing the shot. Some careful cropping at the editing stage will often make up for some careless framing when taking the shot.

Sometimes you are simply unable to get close enough to the subject, and even with maximum zoom it is something less than frame filling. This is often the case with wildlife and sports photography, and when at an event photographing celebrities. Cropping the edges of the photograph effectively extends the zoom range of your camera and gets you closer to the action. It is often the case that there are scenes within scenes, and particularly with wide-angle photography, it is often possible to produce several pictures simply by using different crops of the same shot.

Of course, there is a downside to cropping images, and this is the resultant reduction in the number of pixels. This is unlikely to be of great importance when trimming small amounts of extraneous material from the edges of photographs, but it can limit the maximum print size if a substantial part of the original image is discarded. Many modern cameras have sensors with well over 10 million pixels, which in theory means that you could crop about half the picture and still produce a reasonable A3 size print. No doubt this is possible with some cameras, but bear in mind that it is not just the number of pixels that is important. The image

Fig.3.1 This photograph would benefit from cropping

must be sharp and have a reasonably low noise level if it is to produce a high quality print.

Fig.3.2 The parts that will be cropped are shown much darker than the rest of the image

Fig.3.3 The cropped version of the poppy photograph

The photograph in Figure 3.1 is not bad as it stands but the 3:2 aspect ratio of the camera is not ideally suited to the subject matter. There are some distracting leaves in the foreground on the right edge of the picture, and a distracting stem and leaf in the background near the opposite edge. A better image can be produced by cropping the picture to remove or reduce these parts of the picture. The Crop tool is the tenth one from the top in the toolbar at the left-hand edge of the screen. To use it you simply drag a rectangle that covers the part of the image that you wish to retain. In Figure 3.2 it has been used to select the required area in the poppy picture of Figure 3.1. It is easy to see which parts of the picture will be cropped, as these are shown much darker than the rest of the picture. Eight handles appear on the outline of the cropped area, and these can be dragged to adjust the size of the selection. The selection can be dragged to a new position by using any part of it other than the handles. Right-click on the image and select Crop from the pop-up menu, or press the Return key to actually go ahead and crop the picture (Figure 3.3). Right-click and select Cancel to remove the selection, or press the Escape key.

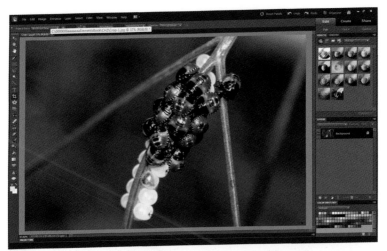

Fig.3.4 This photograph would be better in portrait format

A common compositional error when taking photographs of a predominantly vertical subject is to stick with the usual landscape format rather than turning the camera through ninety degrees and using the

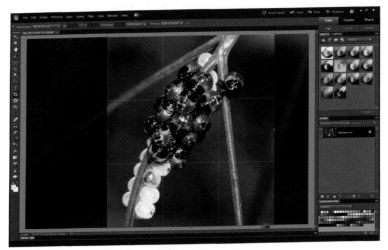

Fig.3.5 The crop lines have been set

Fig.3.6 The cropped version of the photograph

portrait format. The photograph in Figure 3.4 works reasonably well despite the vertical nature of the main subject matter, but it can be easily cropped down to the portrait format (Figure 3.5 and 3.6), which perhaps works a bit better than the original. Cropping from landscape to portrait format results in a huge loss of pixels, with typically about half the pixels being discarded. This significantly reduces the maximum usable print size, so it is definitely better to shoot in the portrait format in the first place rather trying to correct matters later.

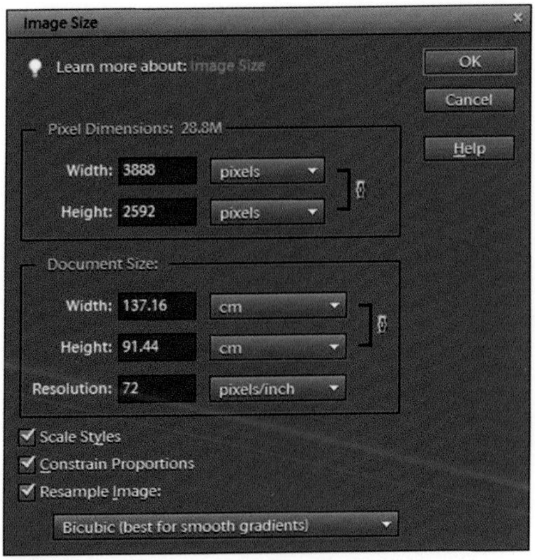

Fig.3.7 The Image Size dialogue box

An Aspect Ratio menu becomes available in the Options bar (immediately below the menu bar) when the Crop tool is selected. By default this places no restrictions on the aspect ratio of the cropped picture, but the other options all restrict the aspect ratio to either a popular ratio for photographic prints (10:8, 16:9, etc.), or to the aspect ratio of the non-cropped picture. You can still drag the cropping rectangle to make it as small or large as you like, but it will be constrained to the selected aspect ratio. This is useful if you need to crop the picture so that it will exactly fit a common size of printing paper.

Resizing

Sometimes it is necessary to resize a picture so that it is a certain size in pixels. These days it is usually resizing in a downwards direction that is required, so that a many megapixel photo can fit into (say) a 400 by 300 pixel space on a web page. In order to scale an image up or down, select Resize from the Image menu, and the Image Size from the submenu. This brings up the dialogue box of Figure 3.7, where the Resample Image checkbox must be ticked. It is also a good idea to have the Constrain Proportions checkbox ticked. It is tempting to simply set the required width and height for the picture, even if this means changing its aspect ratio, and this is possible if Constrain Proportions checkbox is not ticked. Unfortunately, changes in the aspect ratio often produce some odd looking pictures, so it is better to crop the picture to the desired aspect ratio first, and then resize it.

The required new size for the image is set by entering the appropriate figure into the Pixel Width or Height textbox. You only have to enter one figure, because the program will automatically calculate and enter the other figure. There is a menu at the bottom of the Image Size window that offers various resizing algorithms. The ones that are of most interest are the algorithms that are optimised for enlargement, reduction, and smooth gradients. The latter is good for something like portraits where there are gradual changes in skin tones, or landscapes where there are subtle variations in the sky. With everything set correctly, operate the OK button and the image will be rescaled.

If you need to change the size of the picture so that it will print out at a particular size, go to the Image Size window as before, but make sure that the Resample checkbox is NOT ticked. Then set the required size in the Document Width or Height textbox. This will change the notional size of the picture, but it will not alter the number of pixels. Bear in mind that there are usually various sizing and scaling options available when the Print facility is used. For example, if you wish to print the photograph as large as possible on the selected paper size, there is usually a "print to fit paper" option that will do this. You do not necessarily have to bother with changes to the notional size of the picture in order to print it at the required size.

Rotation

In the Image menu there are a number of rotation options in the Rotate submenu. The first three of these rotate the image 90 degrees clockwise or counter-clockwise, and by 180 degrees. Sometimes the image from a digital camera or scanner will need one of these options in order to produce an image that has the correct orientation. The fourth option enables the image to be rotated by an arbitrary amount. In other words, you can specify the degree of rotation and the direction. The small

Fig.3.8 Set the angle and direction of rotation

window of Figure 3.8 appears when the Arbitrary option is selected. Note that you are not restricted to an integer value, and rotation by (say) 2.5 degrees is permissible. It is therefore possible to rotate the image with a high degree of precision, provided it has suitably high resolution. The

Fig.3.9 The horizon is higher on the left than on the right

Left and Right radio buttons respectively give counter-clockwise and clockwise rotation.

Arbitrary rotation can be used creatively, but its main use is to correct sloping horizons and similar image faults. The photograph of Figure 3.9 has a fairly obvious sloping horizon, which is made all the more obvious because the horizon is very near the top of the picture. To correct this type of fault the appropriate radio button must be operated so that the image is rotated in the right direction, and you have to guess the correct amount of rotation. Initially there is a tendency to over estimate the amount of rotation required. In most cases only about one degree or so is needed, and in this case I tried one degree initially. This was fractionally too much, but a reduction to 0.9 degrees produced the desired result (Figure 3.10).

As can be seen from Figure 3.10, Photoshop Elements automatically increases the size of the canvas so that is fully accommodates the rotated image. This leaves four blank areas that must be cropped or retouched. Cropping is quicker and easier, but some content near the edges of the frame will be lost. In the final version of Figure 3.11 I have settled for a small amount of cropping to trim the blank areas.

The Free Rotate Layer option in the Rotate submenu provides another means of rotating the image, and in some ways this is a more convenient

Fig.3.10 A small amount of left rotation has straightened the horizon

way of handling things. The image of Figure 3.12 has a more obvious problem than the previous example. In Figure 3.13 I have zoomed the image out slightly in order to provide some room to manoeuvre, switched

Fig.3.11 The blank areas have been cropped

Fig.3.12 A more obvious case of a sloping horizon

on the grid via the View menu, and selected the Free Rotate Layer option from the Rotate submenu. There is a handle on each corner of the image, and these has been used to drag the image round so that the horizon in the photograph is aligned with the nearest horizontal grid lines. With the picture given a suitable degree of rotation it is just a matter of operating the Enter key to make the change take effect.

Note that with this method the canvas is not enlarged to accommodate the rotated image. This results in some cropping of the image, but four blank areas are still produced. Obviously this factor is of no importance if you will simply be cropping the blank areas, since the missing parts of the picture will be removed anyway. It is less satisfactory if you intend to retain everything in the picture and use cloning techniques to fill in the gaps. It is possible to prevent any loss by increasing the canvas size prior to rotating the image. However, it would probably be easier to use the Custom rotation method instead, or a third method of rotation offered by Photoshop Elements.

This third method is the Straighten tool, which is twelve down from the top in the toolbar. It is great for straightening horizons, but is perhaps more limited in scope than the other rotation methods. It is great for straightening wonky horizons, but it is probably not much use for anything else. The Custom rotate facility is great if you need precision, and the

Fig.3.13 Using Free Rotate Layer to straighten the horizon

Free Rotate Layer method is ideal for any photograph that is well off the "straight and narrow". You can freely turn the image this way and that until it looks right. If you find people have puzzled looks on their faces as they turn one of your photographs this way and that, it probably needs to be reprocessed with the aid of this facility! The Straighten tool is very easy to use. You just drag a line along the offending horizon, and the program does the rest. This includes enlarging the canvas to accommodate the increased size of the image.

Retouching

Photoshop Elements has brush tools that can be used to retouch photographs using traditional techniques, but this will usually be doing it the hard way. The Clone Stamp tool is almost invariably a much quicker, easier, and better way of handling things. It excels at painting over unwanted objects or blemishes by copying from surrounding areas. With a rotated image it can be used to fill in the blank areas by copying nearby material into them. This method has been used in Figure 3.14, which is the finished version of Figure 3.13. Rather than cropping the blank areas they have been filled in using the Clone tool. Also, the bit of bowsprit and rigging on the right edge have been painted out, as have the rear end of a ship a little higher up, and the area of sea wall in the bottom left-hand corner.

Fig.3.14 The finished version of the photograph

Before using the Clone tool a suitable brush has to be selected, and there is a menu of brushes at the left end of the Options bar, and alternative sets are available via a submenu. The default set of brushes is divided into three main groups, and one of these is the round type that produces well defined lines with "clean" edges. The second group produce simple lines but with fuzzy edges. The third group produce textures and effects. The brushes with blurred edges are good for retouching images, as the fuzzy edges often help blend the newly added material with the original image.

A brush with a "hard" edge can be better for fine work where the retouching is being done on a pixel by pixel basis, or something close to it. Filling large areas is quicker and generally more convincing using a large brush, but obviously a small brush is needed for retouching fine detail. It is often a matter of starting with a large brush and moving down to a small one for the final touches. Note that you are not limited to the preset sizes in the brush sets. The Options bar includes a facility for altering the size of the selected brush. You can therefore select any brush of the right type and then alter its size as and when necessary.

In order to paint on the screen using any form of painting tool you hold down the left mouse button while moving the mouse. In the case of the Clone tool an error message will be produced if you try to use it without first indicating what you wish to clone. You do this by first placing the pointer at the centre of the material you wish to clone and pressing the Alt key. Incidentally, when using any form of brush tool the pointer is actually an outline of the brush. You can therefore see the exact size and shape of the selected brush. When you press the Alt key, the pointer will change to a sort of crosshairs sight. Drag the pointer to the centre of the area that will be retouched, release the left mouse button, and then release the Alt key.

By doing this you are indicating an offset to Photoshop. If you dragged the mouse 70 pixels up and 42 pixels to the left, then it will "paint" using material 70 pixels down and 42 pixels to the right of the brush. You are not restricted to copying to and from the areas indicated when setting the offset. It is possible to paint anywhere on the screen using this offset, but with the proviso that the source must be somewhere on the image.

It is necessary to apply some common sense when using the Clone tool. Look at the image to find a source that will convincingly cover the object or blemish that is to be removed. In general it is best to use source material that is quite close to the area that will be covered. Material from further afield often looks as though it is suitable, but when you try it there are problems. In most images there are variations in the general level of brightness from one area to another. This can result in the cloned material being noticeably lighter or darker than its immediate surroundings. Like everything else in a photograph, textures and patterns tend to get smaller as they recede into the distance. If a pattern is obviously larger or smaller than its surroundings it will look like a patched area of the photograph. The direction of any lines in a patterned area is another important consideration. There will often be variations and using cloned material that runs at something very close to the correct angle will give the most convincing results.

It is often necessary to copy from more than one source in order to produce convincing results. Even when dealing with background material, copying a large amount from one area to another can produce a fairly obvious duplication. Using more than one source often produces more convincing results anyway. When using the clone tool it is important to bear in mind that it copies from the image as it is when you start each cloning operation. In other words, you can only clone cloned material by starting a new cloning operation.

This could be useful if you need to move something slightly, but it also means that in most situations there is a definite limit on the amount of material that can be cloned in a single operation. The smaller the offset used, the smaller the amount that can be copied without cloning the object you are trying to cover. Results are often best with a small offset, but a large offset has the advantage of enabling each operation to clone more material. A compromise therefore has to be sought. If circumstances force the use of a small offset, it is still possible to use a small amount of source material to fill a large area. However, it has to be done in several clone operations rather than one large one.

It is desirable to clone material in as few operations as possible as this makes it quick and easy to produce seamless results. In practice this is not an option if a small offset is used, and copying large areas runs the risk of making the use of cloning too obvious. Due care has to be taken when using numerous small cloning operations to fill a large area. It is easier to end up with odd looking repeating patterns than it is to produce convincing results. Varying the direction and size of the offset helps to avoid or at least disguise any repeating patterns.

Alignment option

When trying to make a small amount of source material go a long way it can be useful to remove the tick in the Alignment checkbox of the Options bar. As already explained, the Clone tool normally operates using the offset indicated by pressing the Alt key and dragging the pointer. This offset is used wherever you "paint" on the screen. It can be changed at any time by pressing the Alt key and dragging the pointer again, but it can be tedious and time consuming if numerous changes are required.

Things operate rather differently with the Alignment option switched off. Before using the Clone tool it is merely necessary to press the Alt key and then left-click on the centre of the area that you wish to copy from. Each time you start painting with the Clone tool it will start copying from the point that you indicated. In effect, a new offset is indicated and used each time you start using the Clone tool. Simply press the Alt key and left-click on a different point in order to copy from a different part of the image. Obviously this method can be very useful when it is necessary to copy the same object to various points on the image.

The Opacity control might be better termed the Transparency control, and it gives normal operation at 100 percent and an invisible copy at zero percent. It is sometimes possible to blend the cloned material into the original more convincingly if less than 100 percent opacity is used. With the Alignment option used, it is possible to set a low opacity value and gradually built up the cloned material to the required strength by repeatedly copying it. One slight problem in using less than 100 percent opacity is that it can result in textures in the cloned area of the image being smoothed out. This is almost certain to occur if the cloned material is brought up to the required opacity by copying it from more than one source. There tends to be a sort of averaging process that will certainly alter textures and can lose them altogether.

Healing tool

On trying the Healing tool it will probably seem to work in exactly the same way as the standard Clone Stamp tool. However, rather than just making an exact copy of material it tries to blend it into the surrounding area by adjusting the brightness. In Figure 3.15 I am in the process of using cloned material to cover a light coloured imperfection on the top right-hand petal of the flower. The cloned material is from lower down on the petal and is darker, which has simply resulted in a small white imperfection being replaced with a much larger dark one! However, on releasing the left mouse button the program made a few adjustments, giving the much improved result of Figure 3.16. The cloned area has been lightened to match the surrounding area.

Spot Healing Brush

This tool represents the quickest and easiest way of removing unwanted objects or blemishes from a photograph. It is particularly useful with images that have problems with dark spots caused by dust on the camera's sensor. In order to remove something it is just a matter of painting over it with this tool. It is selected by right-clicking the button in the toolbar for the Healing Brush, and choosing Spot Healing Brush from the little pop-out menu. Note that many of the buttons in the toolbar have alternative functions that can be selected in this way.

In Figure 3.17 I have painted over the dinghy on the left-hand side of the picture, just below the blue fishing boat. On releasing the left mouse button the dinghy has gone and has been replaced by material that is based on the surrounding area (Figure 3.18). In fact in Figure 3.18 I have used the Spot healing brush to remove the mooring buoy on the right, the ship on the horizon, and various boats in the background!

Selective processing

Why is it sometimes advantageous to apply processing to only part of an image? Suppose that you have an image of an object such as a piece of jewellery, and it is on a rather uninspiring background. You might decide to paint in a simple graduated background instead of the

Fig.3.15 The cloned material is too dark

original. This type of thing is much used in advertising, where the main subject is made to look more dynamic and stand out better by replacing the natural background. It can be used to good effect if you produce photographs for online auctions or something of this type.

Having to carefully paint around a complex object is very time consuming. It would clearly be much easier if there was a way of selecting the outline of the main subject and setting everything within it as a no-go area. It would then be easy to paint on the background using the brush tools or using flood fills, as there would be no danger of altering the main subject. Indeed, even if you tried to paint over the main subject it would not be possible to do so.

There are other reasons for using selective processing. For example, sharpening an entire image often works quite well, but it can give some strange looking results with photographs that are a bit "noisy". The noise is most obvious in parts of the image that lack contrast, such as a plain blue area of sky, where the random coloured dots of "noise" do not become partially hidden by the normal textures of the image. There is no point in sharpening these areas since there is no detail to sharpen, and all that will happen is that the "noise" will become about ten times more obvious. Once you have learned to make selections you will soon find plenty of uses for this ability.

Fig.3.16 The cloned material has been merged into the picture

The Photoshop selection tools provide various means of selecting areas that can either be used as no-go zones or as the only areas that can be altered. It is only fair to point out that selecting precisely the right part of an image can be quite easy or very difficult depending on the nature of the image. Something that has "hard" edges that contrast well with the background is likely to be easier than something that has "soft" edges with a tendency to blend into the background. Photoshop has tools and functions that help to deal with awkward parts of an image, but there is no guarantee of perfect results every time. With uncooperative images it is necessary to draw at least part of the selection outline by hand.

In order to increase the chances of selecting exactly the required areas, Photoshop has several selection tools that operate in different ways. The Marquee tools are the most basic, and the rectangular Marquee tool simply selects the area within a rectangle dragged onto the screen. Although it is a pretty basic method of selection, it is one that you will probably use a fair amount in real-world image processing. The Marquee can be restricted to a square by holding down the Shift key while dragging it onto the screen. There is an elliptical version of the Marquee tool which no doubt has its uses, but it is probably not something that will be used frequently. Note that a circle will be produced if the Shift key is held down while using the Elliptical Marquee tool.

Fig.3.17 The Spot Healing Brush has been used to paint over the dinghy near the left edge of the picture

The pointer changes to an arrowhead when it is placed within any marquee, and this indicates that the marquee can be dragged to a different position. The arrowhead is the pointer for the Move tool, and Photoshop Elements is indicating an automatic change to this tool when the pointer is within a marquee. If the Control key is operated while dragging a selection, the contents of the marquee are dragged with it. In effect, a cut and paste operation is performed. Note that dragging the marquee thereafter results in the contents moving with it, and there is no need to hold down the Control after the first time.

Another useful ploy is to operate the Spacebar while dragging a marquee onto the screen. This results in the marquee being moved rather than changed in size. Releasing the Spacebar takes things back to the normal sizing mode. It can be difficult to get it right the first time when using the Marquee tool, but the selection is easily "fine tuned" by switching between the sizing and moving modes via the Spacebar. A further ploy is to hold down the Alt key while dragging a marquee onto the screen. The marquee will then be centred on the starting point. As the marquee is dragged onto the screen, it expands around its starting point.

Making a new selection while an existing selection is present normally results in the original one being deleted. However, it is possible to have multiple selections. Simply hold down the shift key while making a

Fig.3.18 The dinghy has gone, as have a few other objects

selection and any existing selection or selections will be left on the screen. One slight snag with this method is that it is not possible to use the Shift key to constrain the Marquee to a square or circle, since it is being used to indicate that a multiple selection is required.

Selection modes

With a Marquee tool selected there are four buttons near the left end of the Options bar and some menus to the right (Figure 3.19). By default the first button (working from left to right) is active, and this sets the selection process to the mode where a new selection replaces any existing ones. Using the next button along sets the mode where multiple selections are possible. Note that in the multiple mode any overlapping selections are merged into a single selection. If necessary, quite complex shapes can be built up in this way.

Fig.3.19 The marquee options bar

Fig.3.20 The inner marquee is a subtraction type

The third button puts the Marquee tool into Subtraction mode, which enables a "hole" or "knockout" to be placed within an existing selection. It can also be used to nibble pieces from the edge of the exiting selection. In Figure 3.20 I first used the Elliptical Marquee tool to place a large ellipse around the flower, and then using the Subtraction mode a smaller ellipse was placed around the flower. The Delete key was then operated so that the selected area was erased, which is only the area between the two ellipses (Figure 3.21). This clearly shows how the area within the smaller ellipse has been removed from the selection, since this part of the initial selection has not been erased.

The final button is the Intersect with Selection button. Normally two overlapping selections are merged to make one large selection. In the Intersect mode things operate in the opposite manner, with only the overlapping sections being used in the combined selection. This method can be used to produce selections having shapes that are not otherwise possible using the basic Marquee tools.

Mode

Three options are available from the Mode menu on the Options bar. By default the Normal style is selected, and the Marquee tools then work in the standard fashion described previously. As one would expect, using

Fig.3.21 The subtracted area has not been deleted

the Fixed Aspect Ratio mode results in rectangular and elliptical selections having a fixed aspect ratio. This is rather like holding down the Shift key to force a square or circular selection, but other aspect ratios are possible.

The Width and Height textboxes just to the right of the menu become active when this mode is selected. The default aspect ratio is 1 to 1, but any desired ratio can be entered in the textboxes. The third option is for a marquee of a fixed size, and the two textboxes are again active when this option is selected. They are used to set the width and height of the marquee in pixels. In this mode the marquee is produced by left-clicking the mouse. Dragging the marquee obviously has no effect on its size, but instead moves it around the screen. Consequently, there is no need to hold down the Spacebar in order to move the marquee.

Once in position it can be moved in the normal way, and multiple selections are still possible. In Figure 3.22 a series of circular selections were added to produce the desired shape. Then the Inverse option was chosen from the Select menu so that the area within the selection was deselected, and everything else became the new selection. The selection was then erased by pressing the Delete key.

Do not press the Delete key in order to clear marquees from the screen. As we have already seen, this will delete the selected material, leaving the marquee in place. One or more marquees can be deselected by left-clicking anywhere on the image provided Normal mode is selected

Fig.3.22 *This selection is comprised of several circles*

and the New Selection button is active. This effectively replaces the current selection with a new one having zero pixels. In the New Selection and Intersect modes it is possible to remove the current selection or selections by left-clicking within one of the selections. Another method is to right-click on a selection and select Deselect from the popup menu. Note that this clears away all the selections if there is more than one, and not just the selection that was right-clicked. The Deselect option is also available from the Select menu on the menu bar.

Lasso tool

The Marquee tools are adequate for many selection tasks, but they make heavy work of selecting complex shapes. It can be done, but a lot of merging and nibbling is needed to get things right. The Lasso tool is better for selecting awkward shapes since it enables you to draw around the required area. Although it is easy to use in theory, in practice it is difficult to use the Lasso tool with adequate accuracy. Even an experienced and skilled user is unlike to get it right first time. At first it is often a struggle to get anything approximating to the required selection.

A digitising tablet and a stylus is certainly much better than a mouse for this type of thing, and an inexpensive digitising tablet is certainly a worthwhile investment for anyone who uses Photoshop Elements more than occasionally. The merge and subtraction methods work using the Lasso tool, so it is possible to "fine tune" the selection if you do not get it right first time. It is easier to get good accuracy using a zoomed view, so make good use of the pan and zoom facilities when making fine adjustments. Most people find that reducing the sensitivity of the mouse or tablet makes it easier to obtain good accuracy. By reducing sensitivity I mean that the pointing device should be set so that more physical movement is required for a given amount of movement on the screen.

To use the Lasso tool you simply drag a line around the area that you wish to select. There is no need to accurately match the start and finish points of the line. Photoshop will automatically connect the start and finish points. On the other hand, leaving a large gap is unlikely to give adequate accuracy. With practice and the inevitable fine adjustments to the marquee, it will usually be possible to obtain the desired result.

Polygonal Lasso tool

There are two alternative versions of the Lasso tool available, and the first of them is the Polygonal Lasso tool. This is used to draw irregular polygons, and on the face of it the regular Lasso tool is the more useful. The polygonal version draws straight lines between points drawn on the screen, which means that true curves can not be produced. There is no such limitation with the normal Lasso tool, where freehand drawing can be used to produce any shape, curved or otherwise.

However, as already explained, accurate drawing using the normal Lasso tool is very difficult. Even after you have gained some experience it can be very difficult to get really good accuracy without resorting to a great deal of "fine tuning". Drawing complex shapes by picking points on the outline is very much easier. Although it is not possible to draw true curves, a good approximation can be produced using several short lines. In practice, selections made using the Polygonal Lasso tool are often sufficiently accurate without the need for fine adjustments, which is rarely if ever true when using the normal Lasso tool.

Magnetic Lasso tool

This is a sort of semiautomatic version of the standard Lasso tool. As already pointed out, getting accurate results using the normal Lasso tool is quite tricky. Photoshop will faithfully reproduce every little error in your rendering of the outline, and some editing will usually be required once the outline has been completed. The Magnetic Lasso tool makes

Fig.3.23 The Magnetic Lasso tool has done a good job here

life much easier by looking for an outline to follow rather than simply following the exact path of the pointer. How well or otherwise this works depends on how well an object's outline is defined. It should work very well if there is plenty of contrast in shade or colour. If there is no outline to follow, the Magnetic Lasso is not the tool for the job. It is probably not the best tool for the job if there is only an indistinct or intermittent outline to follow.

The flower in the test photograph stands out well from the background, and it did quite a good job of separating the flower from the background (Figure 3.23). Here I have inverted the selection and erased the background so it is easy to see exactly what was selected. It is not quite perfect, but a minimal amount of work would be needed in order to tidy things up.

There are some parameters in the Options bar that enable the Magnetic Lasso tool to be optimised for a given situation. The Width (detection width) setting controls how close the pointer has to be to an edge for the Magnetic Lasso tool to latch onto it. The larger this figure the less accurately you have to follow the outline. Do not be tempted to use a large figure for this setting though. The line might tend to jump off its intended path and onto another outline, particularly if the pointer is allowed to stray well away from the correct path. The Width setting is in pixels incidentally.

The Edge Contrast figure determines the difference in brightness value required for an outline to be recognised. Using a low value enables the outline to be followed even when there is relatively little contrast between the object and the background. Unfortunately, it also increases the likelihood of the line jumping over to a different outline or jumping to any small areas of slight contrast. A small Edge Contrast value normally has to be accompanied by a small Width value and careful drawing of the selection outline. This tool works best with well defined objects and a reasonably high Edge Contrast value.

The Frequency setting controls the number of anchor points that will be added as the outline is drawn. These anchor points are shown as tiny squares on the line while it is being drawn. The higher the number, the more anchor points that are used and the more accurately intricate outlines can be tracked. A high value gives better accuracy with this type of thing, but note that the maximum permissible value is 100. On the down side, a high value might have a tendency to produce rough edges, particularly when used with a low Edge Contrast value.

Using the Magic Lasso tool is again very straightforward. Drag the line making sure that the pointer is kept quite close to the outline you are trying to follow. Release the left mouse button when the pointer is back at the starting point. Alternatively, double-click the mouse with the pointer close to the starting point. Photoshop will then draw a line from between the final and starting points, tracking what it considers to be the correct path.

If things go badly wrong, operate the Escape key to completely remove the line so that you can start from scratch. The last anchor point added can be removed by operating the Delete key, and this key can be operated repeatedly to remove further anchor points back down the line. Keep the pointer still while deleting anchor points so that no new ones are added while you are trying to remove some of the existing points. This tool often gives better results with the pointer kept just to one side of the required path rather than trying to track the pointer right over the path.

Magic Wand tool

With the Magic Wand tool there is no need to draw around the object you wish to select. You just left-click at a suitable point on the image and Photoshop automatically selects the right area. Of course, in reality it is not quite as simple as that, and Photoshop might not get it right. The Magic Wand tool tries to find an outline based on the colour values of the pixels. If there is good colour contrast between the object you are

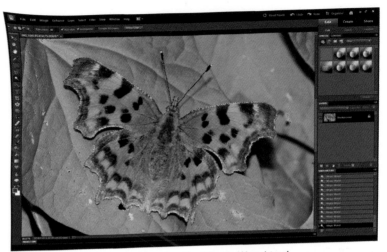

Fig.3.24 A selection made using the Magic Wand tool

trying to select and the background it is likely that the Magic Wand tool will do a good job. Results are less sure if the object blends into the background at some points.

Fig.3.25 Deleting the selection shows that it contains numerous small islands

Fig.3.26 The selection has been cleaned and then blurred

With the Magic Wand tool it is not usually a matter of just left-clicking once on the image and the required selection is made. In the real world it is usually necessary to use the Add to Selection mode and a number of mouse clicks in order to build up the required selection. This was the method used with the butterfly picture of Figure 3.24, where it is the greenery in the background rather than the butterfly that has been selected. Operating the Delete key produced the result of Figure 3.25, where it is clear that the butterfly is intact, but numerous little islands in the selection have been left. These are caused by tiny blemishes on the leaves that are very different in tone and colour to the surrounding area. This type of thing can be cleaned up quite quickly using the Marquee or Lasso tool in the Add to Selection mode. In Figure 3.26 I have cleaned up the selection, inverted it, and used the Average Blur filter to produce a plain green background.

Settings

There are a few Magic Wand settings available from the Options bar. The tolerance setting is important, and it is unlikely that good results will be obtained unless this is adjusted to suit each task. It controls the amount of colour contrast that is needed for Photoshop to perceive the change as an edge. If it is set too low there will be very little selected, but practically everything will be included if it is set too high. A little trial and error will probably be needed in order to find the best value for a given image.

Contiguous

By default the Contiguous checkbox is ticked, which means that a continuous path of pixels is sought by the program, which tries to find an outline. It will also find any "islands" within the outline and automatically subtract them from the selection. The Magic Wand tool simply selects any pixels at colours within its tolerance setting when this checkbox is not ticked. In other words, it tries to find any pixels of the right colour range, anywhere on the image, and it does not try to find outlines.

Anti-aliased

The Anti-aliased checkbox is also ticked by default. This is also available and used by default with the Lasso tools. Anti-aliasing smoothes the edges of the selection or selections, which often gives better results than having it faithfully follow every nook and cranny in an outline. On the other hand, anti-aliasing will probably give less satisfactory results if the required selection genuinely has rough edges. The smoothing will cause parts of the required area to be omitted and (or) material outside the required area to be included. With an area that has a smooth and well defined outline it is unlikely to make much difference one way or the other. Once again, it is a matter of experimenting to find the mode that gives the best results.

Selection menu

Do not overlook the facilities available from the Selection menu. A similar menu is also available by right-clicking within a selection. A Feather option is available when some selection tools are selected, and it also appears in the Options bar when appropriate. It is primarily intended for use with cut/copy and paste operations. There can be problems with objects that are pasted into an image having a two-dimensional cardboard cut-out appearance.

Feathering offers one approach to integrating a pasted object into an image without getting the cardboard cut-out effect. It gives a blurred edge that blends into the new image more realistically, and the width of the feathering (in pixels) can be specified on the Options bar prior to selection. A small dialogue box appears when Feathering is chosen from the Select menu, and this is used to specify a value for the pixel width. This method can be used to add feathering to an existing selection.

There are four options available in the Modify submenu. The border option produces a small dialogue box that requests a pixel value to be entered. Instead of selecting the area within an outline, a band of pixels centred on the outline is selected. The value entered controls the width of the band. The Smooth option does precisely that, and it will smooth out jagged edges in the marquee. The Expand and Contract options simply enlarge or shrink the selection by the specified number of pixels.

One application of the last two options is to take slightly more of an image than is really required for a copy and paste operation. The pasted background is then painted over using the existing background of the destination image. This is not a quick way of doing things, but it ensures that all the required source material is copied with no little bits missing, and the pasted image should integrate quite well with the rest of the destination image. You may find that some selection methods tend to outline slightly too much or too little material. The Expand and Contract options provide quick and easy solutions to these problems.

The Grow option in the main Select menu should not be confused with the Expand option in the Modify submenu. Grow does not expand the border of the selection by a certain number of pixels. Instead, it looks for pixels of a similar colour around the border, and the selection then grows into these. The point of this is to add minor omissions from the edge of selection without introducing extraneous material, which is a problem that is likely to occur with the Expand option.

As we have already seen, the Inverse option simply deselects everything that is currently selected, and selects everything that was not previously selected. It is often easier to select the background and then use the Inverse option to select the main subject matter, rather than taking the more direct route of trying to select the main subject.

Quick Selection tool

As its name implies, this is intended to be a very quick and easy way of making selections. There are actually two tools available via this button, with the alternative one being the Selection Brush Tool. The latter is very simple in operation. You just select a brush, set it at the required size, and then paint over the area you wish to select. Two buttons on the options bar provide addition and subtraction modes. The Quick Selection Tool is an "intelligent" version of the basic Selection Brush tool, which removes the need to carefully paint up to borders. Instead you just click

Fig.3.27 *The outline was found very quickly, but is not quite right*

or drag the brush within the area you wish to select, and the border will be found automatically. As with any automatic selection system, it works better with some things than it does with others.

Fig.3.28 *The Quick Selection tool has worked better here*

Fig.3.29 The selection has been inverted and then blurred

In Figure 3.27 it took only a few seconds to find the outline of the butterfly and delete the background, but some further work is required. Some of the background has been included on the left-hand side, and the butterfly's antennae have been omitted. This tool works best with fairly large areas, and it was difficult to include the antennae even when using a very small brush size. The Magic Wand tool proved to be much better for this task. The Quick Selection worked much better at selecting the blackbird in Figure 3.28, and the original selection required a minimum of "fine tuning". In Figure 3.29 the selection has been inverted and the background then blurred using the Gaussian Blur tool.

The Options bar has three buttons that give New Selection, Add to Selection, and Subtract from Selection modes. There is also an Auto Enhance option that follows outlines better, with fewer rough edges on the one hand, but without taking an over simplistic approach. Results are usually much better when using this option, but it might cause the Quick Selection tool to operate quite slowly.

Layers

A selection can be copied from one image and pasted into another, and I have done this in the jokey example of Figure 3.30. First the selection in Figure 3.28 was copied using the normal Copy option in the Edit menu.

Fig.3.30 The blackbird has been pasted onto a dandelion picture, but it has been placed on a new layer

Then the image of the dandelion and hoverfly was loaded into Photoshop Elements, and the Paste option in the Edit menu was used to add the blackbird selection to this image. The Move tool was then used to shift the blackbird into position. It then becomes clear that the reason for the blackbird looking so happy is that she has spotted a juicy meal!

Paste operations can be a bit confusing for newcomers to Photoshop Elements as the pasted material is automatically placed onto a new layer. New layers are generated by some other facilities of Photoshop Elements. For example, each piece of text that is added using the Text tool is automatically placed onto its own layer. Without realising it, you can soon have quite a large number of layers that Photoshop Elements has generated. As a consequence of this, you find that most of the image cannot be edited, or so it appears anyway.

The point of using one layer per element in the image is that it makes it easy to edit each element separately. For example, text or pasted material can be moved by selecting the correct layer and then dragging it using the Move tool. There is no need to bother about selecting the material that must be moved, since there is nothing else on that layer. Move the entire layer and you move the required elements in the image. There is no need to heal gaps left when the material is moved, because it does not leave any.

Think of layers in terms of each one being on a separate piece of transparent film, with the pieces of film laid one on top of the other. Material on a piece of film near the top of the pile will obscure some of the material on lower layers. If the layer is moved to one side, the obscured material can be seen, but a different part of the image is obscured on the lower layers. Hence objects can be moved around without the need to fill in any gaps left by the changes.

Automatically generated layers can give beginners problems because the new layer becomes the current one, and it is not possible to edit anything on another layer. Attempts to do so either have no effect or produce error messages. Normally it is only possible to edit the current layer. The Layers panel has a list of all the layers in the image, and initially there is just one that is called Background. Any layers that are added by text or paste operations are added above any existing layers, and they are called Layer 1, Layer 2, Layer 3, and so on. The Layers panel can be seen in the Panel Bin in Figure 3.30. The position of a layer in the list is the same as its position in the image. For example, Layer 2 is on top of Layer 1 and the Background layer, and anything on Layer 2 therefore covers these lower layers. Similarly, anything on Layer 3 would obstruct the view of Layer 2 and the lower layers. Apart from the Background layer, it is possible to move a layer to a new position in the list and the image by dragging its name to a new position in the list.

Transparency

A layer does not have to be opaque, and the opacity can be altered by left-clicking its entry in the list to make it the current one, and adjusting the opacity control in the top left-hand corner of the Layers panel. This gives a control range running from zero percent (completely transparent) to one hundred percent (totally opaque). Processing that uses layers is often dependent on one or more layers being semitransparent. A soft focus effect is a good example of this. The Gaussian Blur filter is useful for adding a soft focus effect. It is important to realise that a soft focus effect is not the same as simply blurring the image slightly. Simply adding some Gaussian Blur filtering produces a blurred image and not a soft focus effect. A soft focus effect is produced by having a mixture of a sharp image and one that is very blurred.

Soft focus

A soft focus effect can be produced by having a sharp background image with a blurred image on Layer 1. Low opacity in the blurred image gives

Fig.3.31 The initial version of the photograph

a mild soft focus effect, but the effect gets stronger if the opacity is increased. In Figure 3.31 a sharp background image has been loaded. The next step is to right-click the Background layer's entry in the Layers panel, which produces the pop-up window of Figure 3.32. Here a name for the new layer is entered into the textbox, and the OK button is operated to go ahead and produce the new layer. The new layer will be automatically set as the current one, so the blurring can be added by selecting the required filtering from the Filter menu. I used Gaussian Blurring, and most of the other types are not really suitable for this application.

Fig.3.32 The new layer must be named

Using too little blur filtering is a common error when adding a soft focus effect. If any detail is still visible in the blurred image, mixing it with the sharp image produces a blurred image rather than a soft focus effect. It is preferable to have the broad areas of colour retained from the original image, but all detail must be lost in the blurring. Do not take the filtering so far that a virtually plain image is produced. Adding a totally blurred image with a sharp one tends to produce a loss of contrast with a relatively weak soft focus effect. Something like the degree of filtering

Fig.3.33 The blurred image

shown in Figure 3.33 should give good results. The Opacity control is then adjusted to give the desired effect (Figure 3.34).

The effect can often be improved by slightly increasing the contrast and adding a little sharpening (Figure 3.35). This counteracts the drop in contrast that the soft-focus effect produces, but does not significantly reduce the effect. One way to do this is to first choose the Flatten Image or Merge Visible option from the Layers menu. This merges everything into the Background layer, which can then be processed normally. The image can then be saved in a normal image format such as JPEG or TIFF. Of course, the layer information is lost once the image has been merged into one layer and saved in a standard image format. If you wish to retain layer information it is essential to save the image in Adobe's PSD format prior to merging the layers.

Fig.3.34 The blended image

Graduated filter

Layers and the opacity control are useful for producing effects similar to those obtained by using graduated filters over the camera's lens. For this example a graduated tobacco filter will be simulated. These are

Fig.3.35 The final soft-focus image, with some restored contrast

often used to give an orange/brown tint to the sky while leaving the foreground unaltered. I used the image of Figure 3.36 as the base image, and then added a blank layer by selecting New and then Layer from the Layer menu.

The next step is to add the graduated colour, which must go from orange/ brown at the top of the frame to transparent at the bottom. This is easily achieved using the Gradient tool from the toolbar. The default colour gradient will be shown at the left end of the Options bar when this tool is selected, but the gradient will have to be edited to suit this application. Left or right-clicking the little colour gradient in the Options bar produces the pop-up window of Figure 3.37. There are several preset gradients in the upper part of this window, and the one second along from the left in the top row is almost suitable for our purposes. It goes from red to transparent, and the chequered pattern in the little square is used to indicate transparency is provided rather than a colour. Simply left-click the required preset to select it.

The only problem with this one is that the colour is rather too red, and it must therefore be changed. First left-click on the little marker at the bottom left-hand corner of the gradient bar in the lower part of the window. Then right or left-click on the little coloured rectangle near the bottom left-hand corner of the window, which will launch the colour selection

Fig.3.36 The initial image with no filtering

window (Figure 3.38). There are various ways of setting the required colour, but the easiest is to adjust the big slider control to produce a suitable range of colours in the main panel. Then left-click a colour in the main panel to select it, and click the OK button to close the window. Do the same back at the Gradient Editor, and you are then ready to add the colour gradient.

This is done by dragging a line onto the screen, and the gradient is controlled

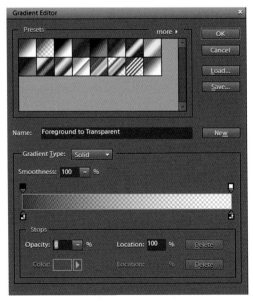

Fig.3.37 The Gradient Editor window

Fig.3.38 The colour selection window

by the position, length, and direction of the line. In this case we need the colour at the top of the picture and transparency at the bottom, and this is achieved using a vertical line, starting at the top. Holding down the Shift key while dragging the line will keep it perfectly vertical. A short line gives a rapid transition from colour to transparency, and a long line gives a gradual change. A short line half-way up the screen therefore gives a rapid transition at that point, while a line from the top of the picture to the bottom gives the most gradual transition. It is really just a matter of using trial and error to find the best effect, using the Undo function to remove the existing gradient before trying another one. Start with the opacity control at about fifty percent, and then adjust it for the best effect once a suitable gradient has been found. Figure 3.39 shows the filter effect that I finally settled for.

Fig.3.39 The picture with the graduated filtering added

Index